MW01644741

A FALLEN EAGLE

A WWII B-24 PILOT IN THE 15TH AIR FORCE WITH THE 450TH BG "COTTONTAILS"

BY

CLARENCE P. COWART LT. COL. AUS RET

© 2009 Clarence P. Cowart Lt. Col. AUS Ret
All Rights Reserved.

No part of this publication may be reproduced, stored in a retrieval system, or transmitted, in any form or by any means, electronic, mechanical, photocopying, recording, or otherwise, without the written permission of the author.

First published by Dog Ear Publishing
4010 W. 86th Street, Ste H
Indianapolis, IN 46268
www.dogearpublishing.net

ISBN: 978-159858-937-5
Library of Congress Control Number: 2010925268

This book is printed on acid-free paper.

Printed in the United States of America

ACKNOWLEDGEMENTS

Special thanks go to my wife, Dixie, who labored with me and encouraged me to write the book. She is to be commended for her efforts to transcribe and type my notes. She made many contributions to the correctness and clarity of the text. I also want to thank her sisters and brother who provided family information and pictures. I am grateful to those individuals who helped to proofread and make revisions to the manuscript, and to Max Dawson who used his ability to improve the quality of some old and faded photographs shown in this book.

DEDICATION

This book is dedicated to the young airmen who gave their lives in aerial combat against the enemy in all theaters during World War II and to the families they left behind.

Contents

FOREWORD

Upon graduation from Texas A & M College in 1943, I went into the army, as a forward observer in the artillery, with the 8th Armored Division. In January of 1944, the division went into combat in support of the final collapse of the Battle of the Bulge. We went on line, without winter clothes, in one of the coldest winters in Europe. The division was in continuous combat until we reached the Elbe River and the war ended in May, 1945. I received the Silver Star and the Purple Heart during this period. From the view point of the front lines of combat, I saw the horror of combat, as no one else could. It is hard for one who fought on the ground to realize what combat in the air was like. This book, written by Lt. Colonel Cowart, has captured aerial combat in a way that helps us understand the anxiety and terror faced by a bomber crew.

The book is historically and accurately written. It shows the anguish that families have to endure, when their love ones are listed as "missing in action," as they wait for months to find out if they survived or were killed. The procedure of identification process the government agencies go through, to make sure no mistakes are made, is explained in detail. Yet, "A Fallen Eagle" is written in a clear and simple way, making it easy to read and understand.

As a bonus to the book, Lt. Colonel Cowart provides information to others who want to search for information about their loved ones who were lost in war times.

Clarence Cowart first came to my Artillery Battalion not long after he came off active duty as a 1st Lieutenant. I assigned him to the ammunition section which was a difficult job that no one wanted. He was able to organize this section and crew into an operation that always had the ammunition on site, on time, and ready to fire. He later served me as Battery Executive Officer and as a Headquarters Company Commander in a later unit. He retired as a Lt. Colonel.

Mike P. Cokinos
Brigadier General AUS Retired

Preface

This book is a tribute to a fallen eagle who gave the supreme sacrifice for his country. This is the story of my wife's brother, 2nd Lt. Clyde Odis Primrose, who was shot down on a bombing raid to Ploesti, Romania, on July 15, 1944. He was co-pilot in the group lead aircraft of the 450th Bomb Group, 47th Wing, 15th Air Force. The plane was a new B-24H with radar. The target was the Americano-Romano Refinery and was to be bombed from 21,000 feet. When the plane was hit, the pilot was blown out of the cockpit and was the only survivor.

Lt. Primrose was a quiet, country boy who grew up on a farm near Hemphill, Texas, in the piney woods of East Texas. He was intelligent and very athletic. He had never been more than fifty miles from home, and did not have a driver's license when he enlisted in the army. By sheer hard work he was able to compete with older men with college educations to successfully complete mechanics school, flight school, and advanced training. By age 20, he had gained his wings and was flying B-24s. This says a lot about the work ethic and schooling in rural America sixty-five years ago.

When the fate of freedom in the world was hanging in the balance, Clyde Odis Primrose, Jr., and thousands of other young men answered the call of their nation. They were ordinary men who were called upon to do extraordinary things. Sixty-five years later, they stand out as America's finest. Many of these men, still in their teenage years, did not even know how to drive. Many plowed behind mules instead of tractors, walked to school, and studied by the light of kerosene lanterns.

This book is a labor of love to record the life of one of the many heroes who flew into combat over enemy territory. This book hopes to give some guidance for children, grandchildren and great-grandchildren of WWII veterans on how, after sixty-five years, they can still research the service of their family heroes. Research is available through bomb group web sites, POW web sites, national archives, and the National Personnel Records Center in St. Louis (most records were destroyed by a fire during the 70's). Information can also be obtained from individual deceased personnel files with the U.S. Army Total Personnel Command in Alexandria, Virginia, and the Depositories of the Individual Army Air Force Command records.

The book is based on over 110 personal letters and fifteen years of personal research. At the beginning, I had only these letters with no information about Lt. Primrose's original crew. A visit to the Air Force Historical Agency at Maxwell Air Force Base provided me access to the original 450th BG records. Using the information I got there, and through many e-mail contacts, interviews, books, and research of records found in Government agencies, I was able to get the facts to complete the book. In addition, my service and retirement from the U. S. Army was invaluable in wading through the technical jargon used by the military, and in making time available for research.

One must remember that researching events of over 65 years ago is difficult, with the possibility of mistakes. My goal has been to tell the story as accurately as possible. Please forgive any errors I have made.

While doing research for the book, I was amazed how things have changed in our country since the period 1941-1945. We now see that talking about God and religion is not politically correct, and should not be associated with the government in any way. The difference can be seen in the religious material furnished to our servicemen during WWII. "Gideons International" was given the task of supplying our troops with small New Testaments. A letter from the president was in front of the Bibles commending the reading of the Bible. Selected hymns and prayers were also included. The military provided every major unit with a chaplain, who had a supply of the "Song and Service for Ship and Field" for both the army and navy. This book contained hymns, a prayer by George Washington, other prayers, and the order of services for various religions. A small book called, "Strength for Service to God and Country" was also provided to the servicemen.

The current trend in our country about God and religion concern me in that we have lost our moral compass since WWII. Our Declaration of Independence on July 4, 1776, recognized the importance of God's hand in the affairs of men. My hope and prayers are that we will again become a strong, patriotic nation that relies on God.

LTC Clarence P. Cowart AUS Ret.

CHAPTER 1

Growing Up

Clyde Odis Primrose, Jr., (called Odis) was born on February 8, 1923, on a rural farm three miles from Jasper, Texas, in Jasper County. Jasper was a very small sawmill and farming town deep in the piney woods of East Texas. His parents were Clyde Odis, Sr. and Leavie McDonald Primrose. Clyde and Leavie were both 18 when they married. Odis was their second child. They previously had a baby girl who lived only eight days.

The Primroses lived on a small farm where they raised dairy cows, chickens, cotton, and vegetables. Times were hard, and like everyone else, Odis' dad had to look for odd jobs to supplement the farm income. He worked as a carpenter whenever he could. He was a hard worker and had grown up working with timber crews and in sawmills.

Clyde Odis Primrose, Sr. truck farming

Three other children, Jack, Dorothy, and Leatrice were born during this period. They moved around in Jasper County several times, looking for "greener pastures." In 1930 the family moved north of Jasper to Sabine County, first to Pineland, then to Hemphill.

Hemphill was a smaller town than Jasper, and was about 10 miles from the Louisiana border. It was a lumber and farming town. Times were as hard following the great depression in this area as they had been in Jasper County. The only industry other than small farms was the timber industry. Temple Lumber Company had a mill near Hemphill at East Mayfield until it burned down in 1937. By that time, the bulk of the timber in the area had been depleted, so it was never rebuilt. Temple continued to operate a larger mill at a small town nearby. The lumber companies controlled about 80 percent of all jobs available, thereby holding the wages very low. They also owned most of the land, leaving only very small tracts available for farming.

After moving to Sabine County, and before Odis finished high school, five more children, Faye, Frances, Shirley, Dixie, and Mary Jane were born into this already large family. Struggling to provide for a family of eleven took a heavy toll on Odis' parents. There was little money available other than what could be made selling vegetables from the farm and the part-time carpenter work his dad did. Only the bare necessities could be purchased. Fortunately, they lived on a farm, they always had food on the table. Odis' mother would also can vegetables and shell and dry beans and peas to prepare for the winter months.

This family was typical of many others during that time. Everyone made shirts and dresses from printed feed sacks. They had very few clothes, and when the older girls outgrew them, they were handed down to the younger ones. Although some families had more than they did, most of them did not.

One of the houses the family lived in at Hemphill was a small three room house which was unfinished when they moved in. The family now looks back and laughs about the house having two door openings, but only one door. The door was moved to whichever opening that had the wind or rain coming in.

The house had no running water or electricity. A wood stove which was used for cooking also provided the only heating in the house. Later, they moved into a larger house where Clyde, Sr. built a fireplace which helped to warm the living and dining area. Cooking and heating required an endless supply of wood, and this job was shared by all the family. The girls, as well as the boys, learned how to chop and saw with a crosscut saw. The younger ones helped hunt pine knots in the woods to be used as kindling.

Clyde Odis, Jr. (center) on farm.

Their water was drawn from the well or carried from the creek. It seems that water was always scarce wherever they lived as most wells were shallow and did not yield very much water. There were times in the summer when the well would have so little water in it that the clothes would have to be carried to the creek to be washed. All clothes were washed by hand using a scrub board, and nearby, on a fire, was a big black pot used for boiling the white clothes. When the laundry was done, the last rinse water was used for bathing the kids. On other bath days, in the summer, the water would be drawn from the well and put in number 3 washtubs, then set in the sun to warm. In the winter, the tubs were set on the wood stove to heat.

During the spring and summer evenings, the family would sit on the front porch where it was cool. The children would play hide-and-seek or other games outside until after dark. When they came in, before going to bed, they all had to wash their feet in a foot tub. The toilet facilities were always typical outhouses.

Each child had specific chores to do each day. Odis being the oldest, was a take-charge person. He gained the respect of the other children and made them do their part of the work. However, he had a habit of picking on the younger ones. When his mother made tea cakes, Odis would stand guard to keep the others from eating them before she finished. He, however, would sneak one for himself every now and then.

There was one time when he could not get any of the other kids to go with him to the watermelon patch for melons. He went alone and brought back two melons. He gave the kids one and took the other one under a tree and ate it by himself.

He and his brother, Jack, did mostly farm work. Along with their dad, they did the plowing with a horse and planting, while the others helped with the hoeing, bringing the produce in from the field, and feeding the chickens. The older girls helped their mom with the cooking and taking care of the younger ones. When their chores at home were finished, and if there was time, all the children who were big enough to pull a cotton sack would pick cotton for the neighbor for a penny a pound.

Growing up in high school, Odis was very athletic. He played basketball, pole vaulted, and ran track. During one basketball game, with the score tied between the two teams, Odis made a shot from the center of the court at the last minute, giving his team two points for the win. He was an average student who did pretty well in math, but was sometimes lazy about his other school work. One report card from his junior year of high school showed all B's and C's.

He was a tall, good-looking young man with reddish hair and was a very quiet person by nature. He had several girl friends, but was very secretive about them. He liked the girls, but between working during most of his free time and having no means of transportation, dating was out of the question.

In his large family, there were always things to do just for fun. He liked shooting baskets with his dad and his mother, hunting squirrels in the nearby woods, and fishing in the nearby creeks. Sometimes they would all sit around eating parched peanuts and making up scary stories. If the battery was good in the radio, they would be allowed to listen to it. The whole family liked to sing, except for Odis, and many nights they would sit around the kitchen stove singing hymns. Odis would intentionally sing off key because he would much rather be doing something else. Although he did not sing very well, he was good at yodeling.

During the summers, Odis helped his dad do odd carpenter jobs in town. His dad worked Odis hard, but Odis never saw any money because it took all they could make together to support the family. All Odis got was the satisfaction of knowing he was helping the family. Not only was his dad a task master, he was also a strong disciplinarian, which was not a bad thing. All of the children grew up respecting their parents and others. Odis' mother was a gentle woman and let the children get by with a lot more than their dad did.

There were times, though, when it was hard to obey the rules. Odis had to have permission to go to town, which was about four miles from the house. He had slipped off to town one day and on the way back, he heard his dad's old car coming. He ran two miles fast enough to beat his dad home.

Most of the time there was no car and the family did not have transportation to go to church. When Odis wanted to go, he would heat up the flat iron on the wood stove, iron his clothes and walk into town to attend services. He was impeccably neat and almost always washed and ironed his own clothes.

After graduation, he worked with his dad. On one job, they worked really hard and were paid with an old car. Naturally, his dad got the car, and all Odis got for his work was getting to drive the car a few times.

There were no jobs and no future for Odis in Hemphill. When Pearl Harbor was attacked, in the fall after he graduated, patriotic fever was running high in the town. In June, 1942, Odis, along with three friends, enlisted in the army. When he was in high school, his dad had let him and his brother, Jack, take a plane ride and from that time on, he was smitten with planes. Odis wanted to be a pilot in the U.S. Army Air Corps and fly like an eagle.

CHAPTER 2

Induction in Service and Home Front Changes

On the morning of June 1, 1942 Odis Primrose and three friends said goodbye to their families and boarded a bus for Beaumont, Texas to be inducted into the army.

Beaumont, a port city near the Gulf of Mexico, differs greatly in terrain from the rolling hills and pine forests of Hemphill. Beaumont, located about 95 miles south of Odis' home, was a large city compared to tiny Hemphill. One can imagine the excitement and the apprehension of these four country boys as they made their first trip to such a big city.

Odis, knowing that his family would be anxious to hear from him, wrote his first letter home after completing his physical. (Author's note: Odis' parents saved all of his letters and they have been reproduced in this book exactly as written. No changes were made to correct spelling or grammar. The letters are included to give the reader a picture of Odis' true character and concern for others. They also show the difficulties the United States had in gearing up for war and the hardships the men had to endure during that time.)

Beaumont, Texas
June 1, 1942

Dear Family,

I just got through with my examinations here in Beaumont and will leave for Houston at 7 o'clock on the train. I don't think Pete will pass. C. B. and Bozo will. Pete's mother had a fit when he left today.

Love,
Odis

Friday before noon
Fort Sam Houston
Co "A" Reception Center
San Antonio, Texas
June 5, 1942

Dear Family,

How are you by now? I am ok, except for the shots I took about an hour ago. I got sick and the sergeant sent me back to the barracks. C. B. Taylor is up here in his bunk and he got sicker than I did. C. B., Bozo and I sleep close together. We will be here about another week or maybe more or less and there is no telling who will leave together or what we will be doing. We won't know where we are going to be sent until we get there. We have had a test and one interview. I signed up as an A. C. mechanic, but the man didn't know whether I would get that or not.

The man that interviewed me asked me all about what I had been doing and I told him, but he didn't seemed pleased so much, except that I told him I could read common blueprints. I may get some part of the Air Corps. I think I still have a chance to take the exam for Air Cadet. They gave us a test to go to officer's training and they tell me if you don't pass it you will never go above Master Sergeant. Well, I will have to go now as I just have three minutes to get up and dress and go about two hundred yards to mess.

Love,
Odis Primrose

After supper
June 5

Dear Folks,

I found out about 30 minutes after I mailed that letter today that we are leaving out. C. B. and I are in the same bunch. Bozo is staying and I don't know when he will leave. I don't know where we are going, but will write you when I get there.

Love,
Odis

In 1942, lives in the small towns and over the nation were changing. Sons and daughters were going off to war. Following a tradition which started during WWI, parents placed a blue star in their window showing that they had a son or daughter in the service. Before long, telegrams began to arrive announcing that loved ones were either missing or killed in action. If the latter happened, the blue star was replaced with a gold one, which meant that someone from that household had paid the ultimate price by giving their life for their country.

Prior to Odis enlisting in the service, his father had gone to work for a government contractor, building barracks at Camp Polk, Louisiana (later upgraded to Fort Polk). The nation was organized so that the most efficient methods were employed in construction. Carpenter crews were organized into groups of approximately 20 men. A crew could build a barrack in one day. Most of the material was precut and ready on-site when the crew started. Helpers were used to hand materials to the crew. All nails had to have all the heads facing the same direction, so that the carpenters would not be slowed down in any way.

Clyde Odis Primrose, Sr. (3rd from left, bottom row) with carpenter crew at Camp Polk.

A large number of older workers left the small towns to work in the refineries, chemical plants, and shipyards at Beaumont and Orange, Texas. Construction grew to the point that cheap efficient apartments were built for workers' families. This enabled the workers to be within walking distance to the shipyards. A forty-eight hour week was the norm. By the end of the war, a ship could be built and launched in just over two weeks. B-24 bombers were turned out one every minute at the Ford Plant at Willow Run in Michigan.

Women were in demand to work in the defense industry, replacing the men who were off to war. The chemical plants and shipyards in the Beaumont, Port Arthur, and Orange area utilized many women in the work force. To encourage workers in industry, the War Department sent ranking military officers to plants to give talks on how important their products were to the war effort. (Author's note: I remember a talk given to sawmill workers on the importance of wood plugs made for emergency repairs on ships in combat.)

The most drastic change on the home front was the shortage of almost everything needed in daily life. The government instituted a system of rationing all essential items. In 1942, the first things rationed were sugar and coffee. They were followed by almost 20 items such as canned foods (Tin used in cans was a vital national defense material.), tires, gasoline, butter, and other things. The government controlled the food rationings by issuing two ration books, one for processed food and one for meats. A family could only purchase these things if they had stamps for them in their ration books. The average ration of gasoline was from three to five gallons a week. In order to get to work, people had to depend on car pooling, buses, trains, bicycles, and sometimes walking.

UNITED STATES
OF AMERICA

War Ration Book One

WARNING

1 Punishments ranging as high as *Ten Years' Imprisonment or $10,000 Fine, or Both,* may be imposed under United States Statutes for violations thereof arising out of infractions of Rationing Orders and Regulations.

2 This book must not be transferred. It must be held and used only by or on behalf of the person to whom it has been issued, and anyone presenting it thereby represents to the Office of Price Administration, an agency of the United States Government, that it is being so held and so used. For any misuse of this book it may be taken from the holder by the Office of Price Administration.

3 In the event either of the departure from the United States of the person to whom this book is issued, or his or her death, the book must be surrendered in accordance with the Regulations.

4 Any person finding a lost book must deliver it promptly to the nearest Ration Board.

OFFICE OF PRICE ADMINISTRATION

Nº 238940 -220

Ration book.

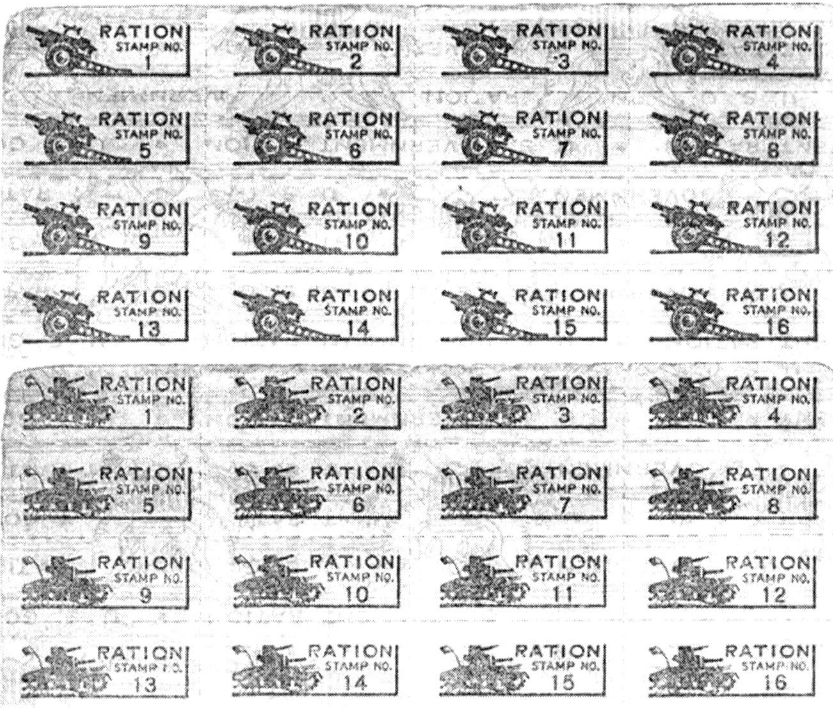

Ration stamps.

The next change in the communities was the collection of scrap metals, paper, string and even tin foil. (Authors note: I remember spending hours stripping tin foil off of gum wrappers and rolling it into balls.) Along with scrap collections, people started planting "victory gardens" in open areas of their yards to supplement the meager rations available.

The government was dependent on war bonds to finance the war machine. School children purchased 10 cent stamps which were pasted into a stamp album. The albums held 187 stamps. When they were filled, they were taken to the post office and exchanged for a United States savings bond which would be worth $25 at maturity. The bonds matured in 10 years giving an equivalent interest rate of 2.9% compounded semi-annually.

Savings stamp book.

The first visual sign of war for East Texans was in the fall of 1943, when a complete armored division went on maneuvers in that area. Tanks were traveling all through the woods and back roads. Anti-aircraft gun emplacements were set in farmer's fields along with various other emplacements. (Author's note: When the soldiers first moved in, I was walking from downtown Pineland, Texas, to my house when I was startled by a machine gunner laying on the ground with his gun pointed at me.)

The community had an outpouring of concerns for the troops and prepared food for them. The Primrose family was no exception. Odis' mother fried chicken and cooked some other things for a group on maneuvers near their house. The men were both surprised and excited to get some home cooked food. Many times food was delivered directly to a tank while it was stopped as part of their exercise.

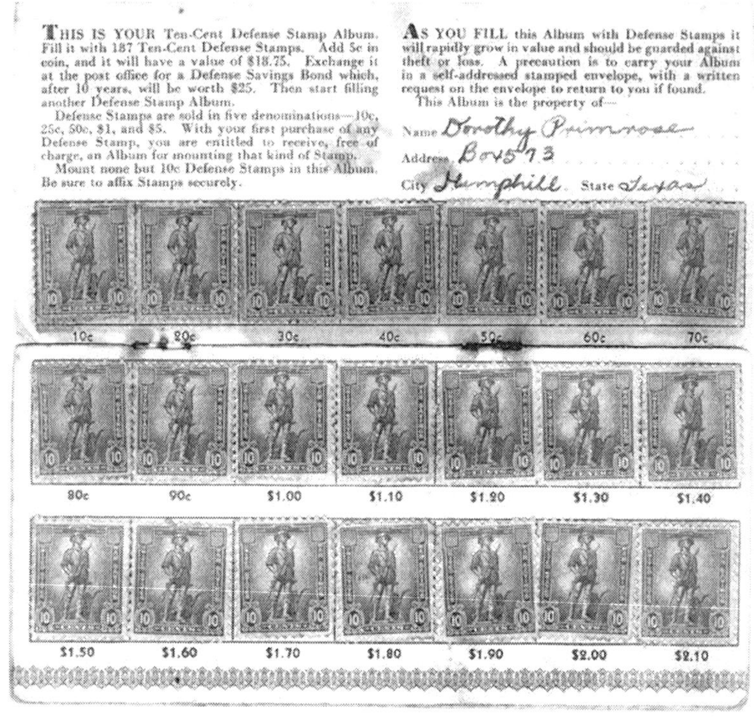

THIS IS YOUR Ten-Cent Defense Stamp Album. Fill it with 187 Ten-Cent Defense Stamps. Add 5c in coin, and it will have a value of $18.75. Exchange it at the post office for a Defense Savings Bond which, after 10 years, will be worth $25. Then start filling another Defense Stamp Album.

Defense Stamps are sold in five denominations—10c, 25c, 50c, $1, and $5. With your first purchase of any Defense Stamp, you are entitled to receive, free of charge, an Album for mounting that kind of Stamp.

Mount none but 10c Defense Stamps in this Album. Be sure to affix Stamps securely.

AS YOU FILL this Album with Defense Stamps it will rapidly grow in value and should be guarded against theft or loss. A precaution is to carry your Album in a self-addressed stamped envelope, with a written request on the envelope to return to you if found.

This Album is the property of—

Name Dorothy Primrose

Address Box 573

City Hemphill State Texas

10c 20c 30c 40c 50c 60c 70c

80c 90c $1.00 $1.10 $1.20 $1.30 $1.40

$1.50 $1.60 $1.70 $1.80 $1.90 $2.00 $2.10

Savings stamps in Dorothy Primrose's book.

KEEP THIS CARD FOR YOUR REFERENCE IN CASE OF DAMAGE

Should your property be damaged through use by our troops, written notice by post-card or letter should be made promptly to:

EIGHTH SERVICE COMMAND RENTS AND CLAIMS BOARD,
Camp Beauregard, Louisiana.

It will receive prompt attention.

CHAYTOR H. RYAN,
Lieutenant Colonel, Q. M. Corps, President,
Eighth Service Command Rents and Claims Board.

Claim information for damages during maneuvers.

Odis' dad was very patriotic and was pleased when Odis signed up with Uncle Sam. The closeness of the family is evident by the volume of letters sent, and responded to, while he was in the service.

When his dad became sick and unable to work, Odis' younger brother Jack was very concerned about the welfare of the family. He decided to quit school during his junior year and go to Beaumont, Texas, to work in the war industry. He lived with an aunt and uncle in Beaumont for awhile to cut his expenses, and was able to provide some financial help to the family.

Odis worried about Jack. He did not know if he could hold down the job because he knew Jack was not physically strong and often sick.

<u>CHAPTER 3</u>

Basic Training and Aircraft Mechanics School

On June 6, 1942, Odis and one of his hometown buddies traveled by bus to Sheppard Field and arrived there about dark. Sheppard Field is located outside of Wichita Falls, Texas, in North Texas near the Oklahoma border. The town was medium size and had been named after the Wichita Indians, who lived near waterfalls on the Wichita River. (Author's note: During my military service the town was nicknamed Whiskey Falls since it was the only wet town in the area.) That area is scrub brush land. It is very hot in the summer and, without large trees to block the wind, is very cold in the winter.

At this time the United States had just begun to go on the offensive in the Pacific with the successful naval battles of the Coral Sea and Midway. It was August when the first ground action began at Guadalcanal. The country was now facing war with both Japan and Germany, which caused mass confusion as hundreds and thousands of men had to be inducted and trained as quickly as possible. Sheppard Field was much like all the camps. The government was building barracks and all the support facilities, while being overloaded with incoming recruits at the same time. It had been only seven months since Pearl Harbor and the government was having difficulty gearing up for war. Adequate facilities and trained personnel were in short supply.

The need for trained aircraft mechanics became critical. Basic training at Sheppard Field was a very unorganized program. The original basic training was supposed to be from 4 to 8 weeks. Odis' basic training lasted a total of 12 days from June 7 until June 19. These men were moved as fast as possible into airplane mechanics school. The original school was cut from twenty-two weeks to sixteen weeks. Since basic training was cut to 12 days, the government integrated basic type training in with the Aircraft Maintenance School. Graduates of this school were sent to air fields all over the United States.

Odis' letters are all used to show what the intense army training was like during this hectic conversion to a war time footing.

After supper
Wichita Falls

Clyde O. Primrose
409 Technical School Squadron
Sheppard Field, Texas
Barracks 167

Dear Family,

How are you? Fine I hope. I am doing ok. We arrived here at Sheppard Field just before dark last night and this is a big place. I guess we will be here at least four weeks. We were rushed off from the other place before schedule. We went to a lecture this evening and he said that we were in the Air Corps and couldn't get out. He said the way each camp got it's men was to send to the reception center for so many men and they sent them the first men on the list and I figure I was lucky to be in the Air Corps, because there are men in our bunch that signed up for infantry, calvary and coast artillery and they came right on to the Air Corps. We still have the chance to take the test to be a cadet. We will be in four to eight weeks of basic training here and then we may be put in the mechanic school here or sent to any place in the U.S. We won't get to leave the camp for 15 days. We have got to get up at four forty five in the morning and then drill and go to lectures the rest of the day.

I would like for you to send me Booley's and Westley's addresses. I might get time to write them sometime.

We came from San Antonio on some great big Bowen busses and stopped at the Baker Hotel in Mineral Wells and ate dinner about four o'clock Saturday evening and it sure was nice.

Well I will close. Write soon.

Love,
Odis Primrose

P.S. I took out $10,000 worth of insurance that cost me $6.40 per month.

Odis often mentions "Booley" in his letters. That was the nickname given to his mother's brother, Luke Edward McDonald. Westley, was his dad's brother. They both were about 10 years older than Odis.

After supper
June 10, 1942

Dear Family.

How are you by now? I am ok. I guess. I have been taking tests, and going to lectures every since I have been here. I can't tell anything about what they are going to do with me and I don't think they know what they want.

Got to fall out.

Well I got back. We can't take a bath except in the morning from four to eight and we are so busy that we don't have time. We get up at four forty-five and go to bed at ten 0'clock. We haven't gotten any laundry done and our clothes are getting dirty. I just had to go to mail call, but I didn't have any, but I was not surprised.

We have about 95 men in this barrack and it is supposed to hold 67. They might ship us out anytime from now on. I wont you all to send all the kin folks my address and tell them to write to me.

We can't leave the camp for 15 days and most of the time that we are off duty we are confined to the barracks. One fellow has a radio up stairs here where I sleep and that helps some. We get up and make the bed, wash, then sweep the floors and then mop them. In the mean time we have to fall out for roll call at 6:30 a.m. We fall out and march up to chow and back and we have about 10 minutes before we march up to the field and take our exercises. After that, we go to a four hour lecture and everybody nearly goes to sleep. Then after chow in the afternoon, we go to another four hour lecture, but later we will drill instead of go to lectures.

Well I guess I will close. Write every chance you get.

Love,
Odis

After supper
June 12, 1942

Dear Folks,

I got your letter yesterday, but I had just gotten a couple of shots about two hours before and I am just now getting able to write. We had to drill this evening and I mean it is hot and dusty!

I got a letter today. I can't write each one of the kids separately because I just do get to write one letter. If we aren't drilling we are standing somewhere in the sun. I don't have time to write much, tomorrow is inspection day and we have to clean up the barracks tonight. Write every chance you get. I will write more next time.

Love,
Odis

Before dinner
June 13, 1942

Dear Folks,

How are you by now? I have just about gotten over the shots and am ok, except I have got sand and grit all over me. A north wind blew up last night and its been blowing dust all over the place. We pulled off our shirts and laid them down while we took exercise and the sand nearly covered them.

C. B. got a report on his examination and this classed him as a mechanic. He and I took the same tests, except I took one radio test. I don't know what they are going to do with me. Some more of the boys are gone now to take more tests.

There are about eight men under 20 years old out of 100 men in our barracks and there are some men 45 or better and some of the men can't march or make up their beds good. As a rule the youngest are 50% better in all ways of the army. Most of the men over 30 will just fill up space and have no ambition except to get back home.

The older men try harder, but they just can't learn. We have a bunch of good officers, but they just keep us marching around and changing their minds all the time.

There's no telling where I will go from here, but I guess I will like it as well as I do here.

I hope you all can keep well and busy and make lots of money. I don't know what I will make the first month. Whatever it is I won't get it all now, it will be held back until I am permanently settled. Send my address to all the kin folks and tell them to write to me. We all look forward to mail call and like to get as many letters and cards as possible.

In all my rounds I haven't seen much of Texas yet. I was on the train at night from Beaumont to Houston and was in one spot of Houston one day and night and then got on the train at night on the way from Houston to San Antonio and from San Antonio up here I couldn't tell where I was or which way I was going, because it was cloudy. All I know is, I passed through lots of towns. We came pretty close to Brown Wood and that was the biggest town we passed.

Well I guess I will close. Write soon.

Love,
Odis

P. S. I hope you can read these letters. I have to write them lying on the bed and I never could write anyway.

June 15, 1942

Dear Folks,

How are you by now? I am ok. I just received your letter and sure was glad to get it. We all go to mail call and are disappointed if we don't get a letter. There isn't much to write about up here. It rained last night and we had to go to two more lectures and drill for about three hours. We are kept busy from 4:45 a.m. until 6:00 p.m. and then sometimes they march us up to a lecture after supper.

I hope you can get the car fixed and keep it running. I guess you can go to town now without everyone knowing it. I am glad Westley is a corporal now, but I don't think much of a corporal. They don't draw much water in this army. Of course it takes you a good while to get to be a corporal. They have to drill their men the way the song tells them and then the sergeants drill the corporals.

You cannot have any suit cases in the army. They issue you everything they want you to have and you can't have anything you can't get into your barracks bag. They issued us one 1 foot wide, 3 feet long and 18 inches deep suit case or foot locker as they call it to 4 men. C. B. and Bozo are here in my Barracks now. They seem to like it as well as the rest. I will try to write to all the folks. I got a letter from Lucy Maye Polly one day. C. B. got a Reporter so I got most of the news. (Author's note: Odis is referring to the Sabine Reporter, which was a newspaper published in Hemphill.)

We haven't gotten any laundry done yet. We have worn two suits since we have been in the army and you can't wash them except in the evening after supper. We have to put them in the barrack bag in the morning while they are still wet and then put them out that evening and when they are dry we can't even iron them.

I don't expect I can send my picture home for awhile yet. I will send one as soon as I have one made.

Don't cut down on the cooking. I can't eat half the stuff we have to eat, but I guess I will get use to it. We have boiled onions, onions & meat and trash and stuff cooked up that tastes all like onions.

I guess I will close. Write soon.

Lots of love,
Odis

Wednesday noon
June 17, 1942

Dear folks,

I hope you are still getting along well. I took another shot about an hour ago, but I still feel ok. We have our easy days when we get shots, if we are not too sick to know about it. We have to sleep under a blanket at night and burn up in the day time. But, it doesn't get as hot up here as it does at San Antonio. Bozo said it got up to 105 degrees at S. A. before he left.

We have had to drill and exercise so much I can hardly walk. We are going on the rifle range Friday and we don't have any guns yet and we are going to have to shoot them. We have got to learn as much in 4 weeks as they use to learn in 6 months.

I hope I am shipped out as soon as possible, because the longer I stay here the more I will have to drill. I don't know where I will go or what I will be doing yet. We have a good bunch of men in our group. If they stay like they are now until they get out of the army, the army will be a good place. I don't know how they will act later on or when they go to town. They have started letting us take showers in the evening now and I think we are going to send our laundry off tomorrow. I haven't seen John Henry Bradley yet, but I don't expect I could come home with him just yet. I am in the replacement center now and he is in the mechanics school up at the other end.

I received two letters from you just a few minutes ago and I read one and I opened the other and a dollar bill fell right out in my face and was I surprised! Some of the boys saw me and said "I wish I could get a few letters like that." I have already signed the pay roll, but I don't know when I will get a payday. It will be about a week or more and I still don't know how much it will be. I received a card from William White and a letter from Ethel McCauley today. I found out that Pete is back driving a log truck.

I guess I will close. I can't think of anything else to write about. Write soon.

Love,
Odis

P. S. I hope you catch more fish next time and get lots of berries to put up this year.

June 18, 1942

Dear Folks,

How are you getting along by now? I am doing ok, except that I have a blistered face. We had another one of those hot days today. We are planning on going on the rifle range tomorrow and I think we are going to have to fire about 16 rounds of ammunition each. I don't expect I will be able to write tomorrow night.

There are lots of buildings going up all over this camp and a big laundry is being built. There's a smoke stack to the laundry that is about 75 feet up in the air and the brick masons are still working on it. It's the tallest building in this camp besides the water tank.

Well, I don't know anything to write about, so I will quit. Write soon.

Love,
Odis

Army life at this point was miserable with the blowing dust, having to go to bed dirty and wearing dirty clothes. Having to wear half washed and dried clothes was a problem especially for someone like Odis, who was impeccably neat. At least at home, he had a stove heated flat iron to iron his clothes, the army provided nothing.

June 19, 1942

Dear Folks,

We went on the rifle range today and it wasn't half bad to me, but you should have heard some of the other boys cuss. We fired 30 rounds each. After we came in this evening, a lot of guys were put on the shipping list. But, I understand it's the mechanics of this bunch. We are leaving at five thirty in the morning for the north end of this camp to the biggest aviation mechanic school in the world. We can take tests for glider pilots, aerial gunners and pilots up there the same as down here. C. B. Taylor had to take the math test over and he may have failed it because he is not on the list. Bozo came up from San Antonio a week later than we did and I heard he was on the list.

I hated that I wasn't shipped out of this place, but I believe it will be better up there. Just two hours of drill a day and the rest schooling. We will be in that school about 21 weeks and by then maybe I will know enough to pass the cadets test.

I received your letter today and one from Guy. I have about got use to getting up early and making up my bed. You like everything you do in the army whatever it is. It is just like play scrubbing the floors if you can get a letter every now and then.

We eat potatoes 3 times a day, but we have an electric peeler in our mess hall.

Well, I don't have any more news, so I will close. Write soon.

Love,
Odis

The firing of 30 rounds on the rifle range would only serve to get the feel of the rifle. The course was called "preparatory marksmanship," firing six rounds in each position: prone, sitting, kneeling, squatting and standing. How to zero the rifle was not taught in this familiarization course.

June 20, 1942

Dear Folks,

I have changed addresses now and I think I will like it better here. There's not so many in the barracks and they are supposed to give us big trunks next week. We are going to get a payday on 10th of July and I think we will get $50.

Bozo is in another barrack across from me. He is planning to go home the 4th. He is really homesick. C. B. is still down in the lower part of the camp and I guess he is doing ok. I never hear him complaining. I may get a three day leave some time this fall and I will come home.

Love,
Odis

June 22, 1942

Dear Folks,

I got a letter from you today which was mailed June 19. It is the first I have received since Friday. I also received a letter from Mamie today.

I have not taken any shots since last Tuesday when I took the typhoid shot. It was the last of three. The Thursday before, they caught me by both arms and gave me two shots.

I sent off my first laundry today and what I have on is dirty. We didn't do anything yesterday and I caught up on my sleep. About all the sleep you can get at night is 6 hours. I think we will start to school Wednesday. Classes will be held in the afternoons. If that is so, we won't have to get up until 6:30 in the mornings. We'll clean the barracks, go to chow then take exercise and drill from 8:30 a.m. until 10:30 a.m. Classes will start at 2:00 p.m. until 10:00 p.m. We have to clean the classroom, and then we have the rest of the day off. We get off Saturday evening at 5:00 p.m. until Sunday at 2:00 p.m. and will get the same time off on holidays.

Most of the men in my barracks are draftees from Oregon, Washington and California. Some are from Kansas and a few from Texas.

Boy, the food we have to eat is just a get by. The men that have the money eat more than half the time at the Post Exchange. I understand now why soldiers use to eat when they went to town.

We have a little more room up here. We can walk between our beds without pulling off our shoes. We are supposed to get a footlocker tomorrow.

Leatrice wanted to know who Lucy May is. She is a girl that works for the draftee board at Hemphill. You all don't know her I don't guess, but daddy and Jack aught to have seen her.

I have gotten 9 letters from you all up until today and I have written that many at least. We don't have a very good mail system here.

I just have 18 more days until payday. There are some who have been here nearly two months and haven't got a payday yet.

Write soon.

Love,
Odis

P. S. If any of you get sick send me a telegram, but wait until I get a payday before you get sick if you can.

June 23, 1942

Dear Folks,

I am doing ok. I did not get any mail today. I saw some airplanes on the ground today, the first since I have been in the army. They don't have many planes here.

This is the biggest aviation mechanic school in the world. We went to two lectures today and one man, a civilian instructor said that this schooling was the best thing a man could take to prepare him for a cadet. This schooling includes the structure, carburetion, and hydraulics on all types of planes and every other kind of instruction on planes. We will be in school for 22 weeks and then I hope I will get a short furlough. I will be in school Friday night before the 4th until 11:30 and then I will be off until Sunday night. Bozo is going to try to go to Beaumont to see his wife, but he will not be able to get there before 3:00 p.m. Saturday, and then will have to start back early Sunday morning.

After we graduate here, we will probably be sent to California. I'm sure we won't be sent anywhere in Texas.

Write soon.

Love,
Odis

June 24, 1942

Dear Folks,

We have from 10:30 a.m. until 2:00 p.m. off every day and that is the only time we have to write letters, shave, take a bath, turn in our laundry and everything else.

If any of you get sick send me a telegram and I will take it to the commanding officer. He will call someone who is the head of the Red Cross in Hemphill and have them investigate. If it is bad enough, the commanding officer will give me a furlough so I can come home. They claim they cannot issue furloughs over the weekend. There are a lot of boys graduating here and are being sent to California without a furlough.

I am beginning to like this place more and more. I have not received any mail since Monday. They have really got our mail mixed up and in a mess. Our entire barrack got 8 letters yesterday and there are usually enough to fill a half bushel basket. Write soon.

Love,
Odis

Monday noon
June 25, 1942

Dear Folks,

I hope you all are doing ok. I wish you would write and tell me if you are getting any of my mail from up here. They would not give us a mail call yesterday and a handful was all that was sent today. I received a letter from you last Friday and I haven't gotten any since.

We went to school 8 hours yesterday just to get acquainted. It's a nice school building. They have all kinds of modern equipment. The school buildings are air conditioned and that helps a lot. We will have 110 school days not counting Sundays and holidays. The two and half hours of drill is worse than the eight hours of school.

The dust is really blowing today. Most of the boys in these barracks are from out of state and they don't like the dust we have all the time. They think Texas is the sorriest state in the union.

Until I get some mail from you I don't know anything to write about.

Love,
Odis

June 26, 1942

Dear Folks,

How are grandma and grandpa getting along? I guess grandma enjoyed the visit with you all.

Yesterday and today we learned about electricity. I don't know what we will study tomorrow. If we learn everything we are supposed to at this school, we'll be worth the money.

I just had a mail call and got the letter mailed on June 23. I also had letters from Pete and Mrs. Doris Robinson.

I don't guess I will be coming home soon. From all the information I am getting, I can't possibly get enough time off to come home until I get out of this school. Write soon.

Love,
Odis

June 27, 1942

Dear Folks,

How are you getting along? I am ok. I will get out of school tonight at 10:00 and get up Monday morning at 3:45 and go to school from 6:00 a.m. until 2:00 p.m. Drill will start at 2:00. I took a test yesterday on electricity and made 88 and will take another today.

I got a card from Grandma and Grandpa McDonald.

I will be out of school next weekend from 2:00 p.m. Friday until 2:00 p.m. Monday. If we get paid the 3rd, I could come home if they would let us ride the train or bus. However, no soldiers can ride the train or bus on holidays.

I sent my first laundry off Monday and still have not gotten it back. Our clothes get so dirty they can't get any dirtier, and I know that for sure.

The dust is still blowing and I guess it will blow all the summer. It cakes up in your ears and makes little mud balls in the corner of your eyes. It gets all on and in your bed everyday. We sweep out about a gallon every morning.

Well, there is no news so I will quit. Write soon.

Love,
Odis

Monday night
June 29, 1942

Dear family,

I hope Dot is getting along better. I know a little about poison oak.

I got a letter from Booley today and he likes the army a little better now. I also received two of your letters today one of them was the one that had the dollar bill in it. I sure can put it to use. We aren't going to be paid until the 15th of July and maybe not then. I hope you all get to go to Grandma's on the 4th.

We are on the morning shift now and we almost went to sleep in class. We took up "Technical Orders" Saturday and "Maintenance Forms" today. We will take up structure in the next phase. (10 days to that phase.) We are on first phase now and like about 4 more days. Third phase will be hydraulics.

I haven't gotten my laundry back yet, but we were issued two pair of coveralls today. The only thing about that is that we can't wear them until the next phase.

Boy, it is getting hot out here. We have a big air conditioning fan in one corner of our school room and one electric fan on each side of the room, but we still sweat a little in there. When we drill in the afternoon from 2:15 until 4:15, we really get hot.

I guess I will start buying me some clothes when I get a payday so I will have something to wear when I do get a chance to come home. You aren't issued nothing fit to wear out in public hardly. I was issued two suits of kaki and one suit was second hand. I got two pairs of G.I. shoes that don't look like anything even when they were new and they can't be shined to look worth anything. I also got a Garrison cap that fits your head like a ball. Most soldiers that you see around town don't have on a thing that the government gives them and the soldiers clothing you buy in town are real high. A cheap suit of kaki is $6.50 and a pair of shoes that we are allowed to wear are $5.95. These caps that are built on a truck driver's style are $3.95 and such as that knocks a soldier's salary.

I guess if I ever get a payday I can send about $20 a month home. Maybe that will help a little. Write soon,

Love,
Odis

July 1, 1942

Dear family

How is your poison oak getting along? Fine, I hope.

I am a tired boy. I mean they put it on our sore backs this evening.

Bozo and I went down to see if C. B. had gotten back and they said he was A.W.O.L. I don't know what will become of him. If he is around Hemphill now, he is there without leave and when he does come back, they will make it hard on him. They are not as strict as the law prescribes, but if you come back in 2 or 3 weeks you get two or three weeks of hard labor and drill and they have your number from then on. He told them when he got the three day pass that his daddy was sick.

I guess we will finish up our first phase Friday and be ready to start on phase two on structure Monday.

It came up a pretty hard wind this evening and filled our barracks with dust.

I don't have a thing to write about so I will close. Write soon.

Love,
Odis

July 2, 1942

Dear Folks,

I hope you are all well. I am doing fine.

When you hear from Thel, send me her address because I want to write everyone I can, so I will get lots of letters.

We are going to take our final test on our first phase tomorrow. It seems that the time is flying by since we are kept so busy.

I will be on barracks guard Saturday. Twelve men from each barrack have to stay in Saturday. I could not go into town anyway and I volunteered to stay. I hope we get to start structure Monday so that we can see some real airplanes. The only real planes we have here are the B-25, the two motor light bombers. The light bombers are the best the U.S. has. They are so fast that they use them in the pursuit of planes sometimes. They have lots of little cub trainers.

I just learned that the rest of my bunch down in squadron 409 was shipped to Panama last night. That is the squadron C. B. was in. I don't guess he got back in time to go.

I have run out of soap.

Love,
Odis

(Author's note: "Run out of soap" was an expression he used to say he had nothing else to write about.)

July 3, 1942

Dear Folks,

I took my final test on the first phase today and I made somewhere around 85. We will start phase 2 on structure Monday and we will wear our coveralls. They are second hand, but they are a lot more comfortable than the uniform.

I got 2 letters from you today. I guess those boys that got in jail will have to learn some sense the hard way.

I have not seen John Henry Bradley since I have been up here. Bozo is leaving for Beaumont this evening. Is Pete still working around Hemphill? I got a letter from him last week and he seemed dissatisfied staying in Hemphill.

I hate to see you sell the car after working so hard to get it. I know you can't get what its worth, but if you have to you have to sell it.

Some of the boys are going home tonight, but most of them are too far away. I am going to plan to come home Labor Day, but I don't know how things will be by then.

I am sorry that you could not go to Jasper on the 4th, but have a good 4th anyway and write soon.

Love,
Odis

July 5, 1942

Dear Folks,

We had an open camp yesterday and civilians were invited out to the camp, but of course they were not allowed around the hangars on the air field. We are not even allowed to go into the hangars. The reception center put on a parade on the drill field. A staff sergeant jumped out of a B-18, but I did not see him.

I went to the service club last night to a free picture show. It was a good show.

Have you heard from Booley lately? I got one letter from him over a week ago. He may be shipped to Australia anytime now. They claim that they won't do that, but it doesn't take much experience to do what he is doing and he can learn just as fast over there and maybe do some good. They sent the boys that came in when I did to Panama and there are plenty of soldiers that say they know of a few that have been shipped to Australia after about four weeks of drill.

One of our instructors told us that a boy that had finished school about a month ago wrote him that he was to start drawing foreign pay the Sunday after he wrote. He was about to be shipped out. By the time I get out of school I might not have to work on the line very long before I am shipped out.

They have just begun to let men go on the fields and learn as they go along. The crew chief has about eight men and he can get to know the men pretty fast. The ones that get to go to school will get all the ratings first. Write soon.

Love,
Odis

July 7, 1942

Dear Folks,

We started studying structure yesterday. We rolled onc of the planes out of the hangar and looked it over. I got in while the others pushed the plane. I worked the brakes and I mean they have brakes! The one we looked at was just like some they brought up from Hawaii. I looked at one of them and it had a bullet hole that went through right behind the gunner. Our instructor said they had two more planes that were full of holes. Of course none of these planes are being flown now.

We looked at a P-37. They are good ships, but the pilots set so far to the rear that they can't stand any fast movements and the government grounded it.

I just finished one and a half hours of daily work. I am getting behind with my letter writing. I got a letter from Grace Wilshire, Grandma Primrose, Curtis and Maye and one from you all yesterday and one from Booley, Grandma McDonald and another from you today. I am glad you do not have to sell the car. I will make it some how until payday, whenever that is. We haven't signed the payroll yet.

I will have to go to school some more. Write soon.

Love,
Odis

July 9, 1942

Dear Folks,

How are you all doing by now? I am ok. I have not gained any weight since I have been in the army, but I haven't been sick at all.

I signed the payroll this morning. I guess I will get a payday some time within the next month.

I am glad you are getting to can lots of stuff, because I know it will come in handy this winter. I got a letter from you yesterday, but didn't have time to answer it. There is no news, so I will close. Write soon.

Love,
Odis

July 15, 1942

Dear Folks,

I received a letter from you yesterday and one the day before. I did not have any envelopes so I didn't write. We got paid today and I got $33.00. They took out two months insurance and other things.

We are finishing the structure phase now. I have crawled all over every plane in the hangar. I didn't know that an airplane had so many parts until I started this phase. Now, I understand why it costs so much to build them.

The biggest planes they have here are the B-25 bombers and we aren't allowed around them. I don't guess I will get to ride in a plane for a good while yet.

I got a letter from Booley the other day. He seemed ok. I have not seen C. B. Taylor. I don't know what became of him.

I am sending you $15.00 in a registered letter this afternoon. I wish I could send more, but I just can't spare it. Write soon.

Love,
Odis

The army pay in 1942 was $50/month for a private. The net pay of $33.00 was not very much. Sending $15 or $20 home would leave him almost nothing to pay for the personal things a soldier had to buy, but his family came first.

July 16, 1942

Dear Folks,

We took our final exam on the second phase today and I made 80. We will start on the hydraulic phase tomorrow. I went over and put my application in for flying cadet this afternoon. I have been waiting nearly a week for them to write my "General Classification" grade and it came in today. I made 125 out of 150. The least you can make to apply for flying cadet is 110. If I pass the mental and physical test, I will send you some papers to sign. All that I am learning in this school will help me out if I get to be a cadet.

I am sending $20.00 in this letter and maybe it will help straighten up a few bills.

I have not seen a watermelon this year and I sure wish I had about a half of one right now. We had cantaloupe for breakfast a couple of mornings.

Boy I mean it's really hot here. We have cool water at school but it is hot in the barracks. We have not had rain in nearly a month out here. Booley said it is awfully hot and dry where he is too. Write soon.

Love,
Odis

The application for flying cadet training was the first of many steps for Odis to begin pilot training.

July 21, 1942

Dear Folks,

How are you doing by now? I am doing ok, except for a sore throat and bad cold. I have an appointment with the dentist next Tuesday.

I received a letter from you yesterday and one a few minutes ago. I also got a letter from Westley. He didn't have any important news. I have been so busy I haven't written any letters hardly in the last two weeks. I went to town Saturday night and Sunday and didn't get to write then. Wichita Falls is a good size town, a little bigger than San Augustine and looks about like San Augustine, but there are not shade trees out here.

I ate turkey for dinner here in camp Sunday, but the way it was cooked was not so good.

I haven't seen C. B. since he went home. Bozo's wife is coming up here to live next weekend. I don't know how she is coming, but she is.

I don't have anything to write about. Nothing ever happens around, just the same old things all the time.

Love,
Odis

July 24, 1942

Dear Folks,

How are you by now? I am as well as usual. I got a letter from Dixie the other day.

I was standing in chow line this morning and I looked up and saw John Henry Bradley walking down the sidewalk toward me. He would not have seen me if I had not spoken to him.

Well, I am going to plan to come home Labor day. That may be my last chance to come home. I will not get a furlough until I am permanently stationed and I may be in California by then. Write soon.

Love,
Odis

July 26, 1942

Dear Folks,

How are you? I am doing fine. I have been asleep nearly all day. I thought I would try to write if I can think of anything to say.

I like Mondays and Tuesdays in hydraulics. Next I will start studying propellers. There was one boy from my barracks who was called to take his cadets test, but he had his application in before I did. If I take the examination soon and pass it, it may be six months before I am called. There are lots of boys waiting now. That's the reason I put my application in so soon.

I bought myself a suit of kakis the other day that cost $6.24 and paid $1.00 for a garrison cap. I am going to try to get me some shoes next payday.

The reason I don't write more often is because I don't have time and most of the time I don't have anything to write about.

Bozo's wife was supposed to have come in yesterday, but I haven't seen Bozo since yesterday evening and I don't know whether she did or not.

I got a letter from Pete Saturday and he thinks he will be drafted in about a month, but I don't think they will take him.

They voted this county "dry" yesterday. I guess there will be some terrible bootlegging going on around here.

Well, I have run out of soap, so will close. Write soon.

Love,
Odis

July 27, 1942

Dear Folks,

How are you getting along? I am fine except my nose bleeds nearly all the time.

I got my notice this evening to take my cadets examination tomorrow at 12:30. There have been several to take it but they all failed it.

I was listening to a radio program from Kessler Field in Biloxi, Mississippi. They said that they turned out a hundred mechanics every 10 days and there are a thousand turned out here every 10 days. This school is supposed to be the largest of its kind in the world.

Bozo's wife came in Saturday night and I mean he is really happy now.

I received your letter this evening. We have cake and ice cream every now and then. We had steak for dinner today and beans for supper and of course we have potatoes every meal. The worst chow we have now is the days they try to feed us some kind of fish that you can smell a hundred yards away from the mess hall and by the time you get there, you can't take one bite of it. We had fried chicken Sunday for the first time since I have been in the army.

I saw a small airplane up on the field today. It had about a twenty five foot wing spread. It was so small I don't see how it could fly. Our instructor said that it didn't have any foot pedals. The wheel on the stick turned the rudder and ailerons at the same time.

I have run out of soap. Write soon.

Love,
Odis

July 29, 1942

Dear Folks,

I received a letter from you yesterday and one from Dixie today. I finished Hydraulics yesterday. I haven't seen my card yet all I know is that I passed and had 80 or better average for daily work. I took the aviation flying cadets test yesterday, but I failed it. It will be a whole 30 days before I will be allowed to take it again. Or, I can sign up for enlisted pilot and not have to take a test.

We were issued another suit of kakis today. I have 4 suits now and if I get paid on the first, I am going to get a cap and a pair of shoes.

I don't imagine I can make it home Labor Day. We leave the school room 10:00 p.m. Saturday night and have to be back in the school room at 6:00 a.m. Tuesday. If I did come, I would not have very long to stay.

Well, we have the same old things to do every day. I guess I will quit and get my lesson in propellers. The governor on the propeller has 117 parts in it. Of course, we don't have to learn all those parts because the whole thing isn't any bigger than your two fists. Write soon.

Love,
Odis

Odis took the aviation cadet test to begin pilot training which would lead to a commission as a 2nd Lieutenant upon completion. Enlisted pilot training would lead to a commission as a Flight Officer (Warrant Officer) upon completion.

August 2, 1942

Dear Folks,

How are you getting along? I am doing fine. I went up to the service club last night to see Jimmy Lunceford and band, the all colored band. It was sponsored by the U.S.O just like all the shows at the service club.

I guess the maneuvers are getting in a big way down there by now. I really feel sorry for the soldiers on maneuvers because I know how tough it is here and it must be much worse in camp.

There are only two jeeps around here. They have put women to driving all army vehicles including medium size tanks.

I am in group B in school and we alternate every week from morning to evening shifts. This is our long weekend. We were off yesterday evening at 4:30 and we start to school at 2:00 p.m. tomorrow. We still have to get up at 6:30 in the morning.

I think we are going to get paid Tuesday. We are supposed to get paid on the first of every month, but they haven't got all the men and names straightened out yet.

It is still dry and dusty. We have just had one or two showers in about 6 weeks.

Send me the Sabine Reporter every chance you get. Write soon.

Love,
Odis

The Aircraft Maintenance School was still adding basic training tasks to make up for not having regular basic training.

August 4, 1942

Dear Folks,

How are you by now? I am doing ok. I finished test blocks and I had a 91 final average. There was only one guy in my barracks that had a better grade. I am working on a P-40 now. We are just making inspections. It does not have a propeller and it is not in shape to run. Before we get out of "single engines" we are going to get an airplane that will run. It looks like I am going to get to stay here and finish school. There are a few going to be shipped out within a week.

We had turkey for dinner today, but it didn't taste very good. They don't know how to cook around here.

I guess I will wait until I get to another place to have the pictures made.

I wish I had something to write about, but nothing ever happens around here. I will close. Write soon.

Love,
Odis

August 5, 1942

Dear Folks,

How are you getting along? I am doing fine. It is hot now as it has been since I have been here.

I got a letter from you and one from Thel today and one from Dixie yesterday. I don't think you get my letters as fast as I get yours. If you mail them one day, I get them the next.

I don't know if we will get paid today or not. I went to the dentist yesterday and today and got a silver crown on one of my jaw teeth. I don't like it so well, but I guess it is better than it was.

I hear we are going to get rifle drill, gas mask drill and every other thing they can think of for us to do. We have been practicing guard duty. Write soon.

Love,
Odis

August 7, 1942

Dear Folks,

How are you doing? I am fine. Boy it is hot here now. It was 105 degrees in the school room one day this week and close to that every day.

I got a letter from Booley night before last. He seems to be doing ok.

I guess I will finish another phase tomorrow and start "Instruments" bright and early Monday morning.

I am going to send a little money home if I can ever get a chance to get a money order. I am sending some papers home to get signed and notarized for enlisted pilot.

I am going to try to go to town this Sunday. About one time a month is about all I can go.

Well, I will try to write more next time. Write soon.

Love,
Odis

August 9, 1942

Dear Folks,

How are you getting along by now? I am doing fine. I am in town now in the U.S.O. I finished up the propeller phase last night and had an 85 average test grade over all.

I just finished a ham and egg breakfast.

About the enlisted pilot papers, I will also have to have a transcript of my high school credits and three letters of recommendation.

I am going to try to round up a watermelon today. I have just about forgotten how they are supposed to taste.

I don't have any news so I will close. Write soon.

Love,
Odis

August 12, 1942

Dear Folks,

I received your letter today with the papers in it. I received a stationary kit from Dixie. I ran into old Buck Mills today. He is going to school here and is just three phases behind me. I was really surprised to see him. He has not had a payday yet and I am going to take him to a picture show.

We are drilling with our gas masks these days. We have to stop and put them on when they call out "gas" real loud.

I went to town Sunday and I went all over Wichita Falls. I went skating and bowling. Some more guys and I bought a watermelon and ate it. I found me a girl Sunday evening and we went to a show. I don't know whether she will be my girl next weekend or not.

We are studying instruments now and I mean they are really complicated.

I wrote Westley a letter right after I received one from him. I expect he has received it by now. I owe Thel, Dixie, Booley, Grace Wiltshire and Lucy May Polly a letter each.

I bought myself a pair of shoes yesterday evening. They cost $5.00.

Some of the boys down in the reception center are wearing short pants these days. I don't know what they will have the boys doing next.

Well, I will close. I am trying to write on this paper Dixie sent me and I don't know where to write. Write soon.

Love,
Odis

August 18, 1942

Dear Folks,

How are you getting along by now? I am doing fine. I went to town over the weekend and didn't get a chance to write you. I received the registered letter with the papers today. Anytime I take them over to the orderly room, I can take the physical examination. I am going to wait until next week to take the physical, because I will have to have my eyes dilated and won't be able to see very well for 24 hours.

Bozo got a letter form Onie B. Morrison and she said that C. B. Taylor was in California and was a Pfc. That was the first I had heard from him since he was in Hemphill.

I met another boy that I went to school with that lived in Geneva. He is in the same squadron as Buck Mills.

The weather has changed a little here. We got a little rain Saturday and the nights have been cooler the past two or three days.

I got a letter from Booley and one from Westley the other day. They both are doing o.k. Write soon.

Love,
Odis

P. S. You can send me my watch if you get time and it is not too much trouble.

August 19, 1942

Dear Folks,

I received your letter today. I am getting along fine. You seem to be having good luck fishing this summer. Are there any squirrels this year? I don't expect I will get to come home to kill any of them, but I never give up hope.

I can't seem to get around to having a good picture made of myself. About the cheapest ones are $3.00 each. I have two or three Kodak pictures made that I will send to you when I get them. I sent Booley one just like I sent you.

They are going to start a glider mechanics school here that will be a four phase school. They haven't brought in any gliders yet, but they will. I have not seen a glider.

Write soon.

Love,
Odis

August 25, 1942

Dear Folks,

How are you by now? I am doing fine.

I guess Jack and the girls are back by now. I know they had a good time while they were down there. Is Bruce still farming? I haven't heard from Westley in about a week and a half. I got a letter from Booley yesterday and one from Dixie today.

We went on a hike this evening after school. We ran about half the way then walked the other half.

I ran up with a Buckley boy (T. J.) from Hemphill the other day and he told me that a McCloud boy was here at Sheppard Field.

We are studying engines now. The first three days we studied the R-2600 radial engine. It is used on the B-25 which is the medium bomber that bombed Tokyo. Today we are studying the Allison. It is used on P-36, P-37, P-38, P-39, P-40 and others. We saw three B-24's yesterday. They were the first I have seen. They are just about as good as B-17 (4 engine) plane. B-18 is a big 2 engine plane, but they don't use them any more. They have several P-40 planes up in the single engine hangar.

I will close for now. Write soon.

Love,
Odis

August 27, 1942

Dear Folks,

How are you doing? I am fine. I received your letter this evening after I got back from a 3 mile hike. We have to go without hats and shirts and I got two blistered shoulders.

There must be lots of muscadines this year for you to have gotten so many.

What day is school going to start down there? I didn't know what school was until I started here. I never studied half as much while I was in high school. We have a five minute break every hour sometimes and one 10 minute break for each four hours. Everyone is talking about or discussing the lesson during breaks and you stay mixed up all the time. I never knew they could get so many parts in one little place until we started studying these engines.

It tried to rain a little last week, but it looks like it will never rain here now. Write soon.

Love,
Odis

August 28. 1942

Dear Folks,

Hope you are doing ok now. I am fine.

You seem to be putting up plenty of muscadine jelly now. If you run out of everything else, you can always eat bread and jelly.

Did you show the Wiltshire girl my picture? She asked me in two or three letters to send her one of my pictures. I also asked her to send me one of hers, but I don't have one of her and I don't think she really wants one of mine.

You said Mary Jane was jabbering all the time. I guess she will talk plain before I get to come home. I guess all the kids are raring to get back to school.

Well, I guess we will get paid next week if they don't take a notion not to pay us.

I have not taken my physical examination for enlisted pilot yet. I am going to take the cadets test again next week and if I fail it again I will go ahead and be an enlisted pilot.

I don't have any news, so I will close. Write soon.

Love,
Odis

August 31, 1942

Dear Folks,

How are you doing by now? I am fine. I got paid this morning ($40.59) and am sending $15.00.

I saw the McAlland boy yesterday. He said he saw daddy in Hemphill while he was on his furlough.

The weather is not quite so hot now. Yesterday and today have been just about right, although it has not rained yet.

Well, I guess we will finish another phase tomorrow and then start electricity and after that comes carburetion. We have passed the half-way mark now. Colonel Clagget came in. It was the first time I had ever seen him.

Write soon.

Love,
Odis

September 2, 1942

Dear Folks,

How are you getting along by now? I am doing ok.

My average grade for engine repair was 85. That makes three straight phases that I have had 85 or better in and I should get a Class A pass now.

I received your letter just a few minutes ago. The pictures looked natural. If you have any more made, send me the negatives. I can get some made from them here in town.

I received the diary from Mr. and Mrs. Walker yesterday.

Well, I don't have a thing to write about, so I will have to close. Write every chance you get.

Love,
Odis

September 3, 1942

Dear Folks,

How are you doing by now? I am doing fine. I received your letter just a few minutes ago. I took the cadets exam over yesterday and failed it. It was all together different from the other one. I went over and got my papers fixed up for enlisted pilot this morning. I will take the physical tomorrow or the next day. If I pass, the sergeant said that I would probably ship out within three weeks. They have cut the phases down to eight days each. We get Labor Day off and that will cut this one down to seven.

Bozo's mother and sister are up here to see him.

It came a big shower last night and it is still cloudy, but the ground has already drained off.

I got a letter from Mamie and Auntie today. They are getting along ok. Write soon.

Love,
Odis

September 10, 1942

Dear Folks,

How are you by now? I am fine. I had my eyes dilated Tuesday evening and I haven't been able to see for the last two days.

I got in camp here Tuesday morning at 6:00. The taxi driver stopped in his home town (Kilgore) and stayed too long. I missed roll call here in the barracks, but I got to school in time for roll call there. When they called my name here at the barracks, someone hollered out, "Here" and they did not know I wasn't here. I got by with the pass I had to turn in at the orderly room and everything turned out o.k.

I passed the physical examination and I will go up before the boards in a few days. I will ship out in a week or so.

There was only one guy in my barrack that had every heard of a muscadine. They said they were concord grapes.

I got the pictures that you had sent me. Write soon.

Love,
Odis

Odis was able to go home for the first time on the long Labor Day holiday, but he was late returning. He was saved from getting in trouble by someone answering for him. This is an old trick in the army.

September 13, 1942

Dear Folks,

How are you doing? I am fine. I haven't heard from you since I was at home.

I finished another phase Friday and I made an 85 average, the same as I made in engine repair. I have had an 80 proficiency and I made 96 on the final exam in both phases.

I went up this morning and sat in the shade and watched Buck Mills and two of the other boys drill. They had to drill from 8:00 this morning until 11:30 for missing bed check Monday. I was lucky that I got by with it.

I haven't heard any more about the enlisted pilot business. I guess they will call me up to go before the board sometime this week.

We had yesterday afternoon off. We took our exercise and made another cross country run yesterday morning. I caught up with my sleep yesterday evening and last night.

Have you heard from Booley lately? I have not heard from him for quite awhile. Write soon.

Love,
Odis

P.S. Have you received anymore of those family letters yet?

September 17, 1942

Dear Folks,

How are you by now? I am doing fine. We have had to make two three mile runs this week and we have a five mile hike scheduled for tomorrow. I got my notice to report to the cadet board tomorrow and I will miss the hike.

My laundry has not come back yet and I don't have any clean clothes to wear when I meet with the board in the morning. All I can do is hope that it comes in this evening. I heard that the next bunch of cadets and enlisted pilots, trained in the same bunch, will be shipped to California. That would be just my luck.

Nothing ever happens around here so I will close. Write soon.

Love,
Odis

September 18, 1942

Dear Folks,

I have got to have three more letters of recommendation. The three that I had were all typed identically. They have to be worded differently.

I have to go to school now so I will close. Write soon.

Love,
Odis

P.S. Rush the letters

September 20, 1942

Dear Folks,

How are you by now? I am doing ok.

A rain came in from the North night before last and rained all day yesterday. I slept under two wool blankets, one sheet and a comforter last night.

We start on our six hour shifts next Wednesday. I will be going to school from 6:00 until 12:00 at night. We are studying carburetors now and I have made pretty good daily test grades. We have had 4 tests and I made 85-86-90-94. We also had a semi-final and I made 94 on it.

I got a letter from Mamie and she said that the house where they live might be sold and they would have to move.

I wrote S. T. a letter the other day. I guess Eustice plans on owning half of Beaumont pretty soon. He bought a FHA house he probably wont ever get paid for before he moves. Write soon.

Love,
Odis

September 22, 1942

Dear Folks,

How are you by now? Fine I hope. I am ok. I finished another phase. I made 88 on the final today. I will start to school tomorrow night at 6:00 and get out at 12:00, eat breakfast at 1:00 a.m. and sleep until 10:00 in the morning.

I received the letters of recommendation today and I hope I have it straightened out now. They wouldn't take the one George Russel wrote, but the other two were ok. The one that Harry Becton wrote made three that were ok.

Well, we start putting what we have learned into practice for the next 24 school days, which includes test blocks, single engines, and multi-engines.

Kenny Baker is putting on a show up at the service club tonight, so I guess I will go to see it. I don't have to get up until 8:00 in the morning. We have another one of those cross country runs scheduled for tomorrow.

I still have not heard from Booley in nearly a month.

Write soon.

Love,
Odis

September 30, 1942

Dear Folks,

I received your letter today. Well today is payday and it didn't come a bit too soon. I guess it will be the last one in this field. I don't know what I'll do about having the pictures made. It takes two weeks to get them and I don't know whether I will be here that long or not. We had roll call in bed this morning and I didn't get up until 11:00 a.m. We have quite a bit of time now.

I got a letter from Mamie and she said they were going to have to move. I guess they won't ever be satisfied until they get back up to McElroy.

Have you heard from Booley yet? I have not heard from him since I was home. I haven't written to him. I don't know whether he has been shipped out or not. I haven't heard from Lawrence. I don't guess he has my address. I wrote to S. T., but she has not answered it yet.

I guess the Morrison boy is greatly enthused about going into the army, but they will take the starch out of him in about a week.

Have you heard whether Pete has gone up to be examined yet? He said he was going to be sometime soon.

Well, I don't have any news so I will close. Write soon,

Love,
Odis

October 10, 1942

Dear Folks,

I received your letter yesterday. I am getting along ok. Today is the last day of "single engines". About all we do is make inspections. I ran one plane eight minutes and that's all. We are working on an old P-40 and it doesn't have a prop on it. We ran a P.T. We had to let the oil pressure get up, then run it up to about 1400 RPM and then change propeller to low pitch to take the load off the engine. Then we had to check right and left magnetos and then we ran it back down to about 700 RPM and checked for both and then ran it up to 1800 RPM just for fun. When you get it up that high, it looks like it is fixing to jump the blocks.

I haven't heard any more about shipping out, but I think I will get my A. M. diploma before I am shipped.

Well, I don't ever have any news, so I will close. Write soon.

Love,
Odis

October 13, 1942

Dear Folks,

How are you by now? I am doing ok. I made an 85 average in single engine branch. We are working on an A-18 for the first four days in multi-engines and on a B-25 the last 4 days. Each man gets to preflight the B-25 and maybe the A-18.

I am going to try to get a furlough after I graduate if I don't ship out before. If I do I will be home Wednesday night or Thursday.

Did Booley get to come home? I never did find out. I still have not heard from him.

We did a five mile hike this evening.

Well, I can't think of a thing to write so I will close and write more next time. Write soon.

Love,
Odis

October 15, 1942

Dear folks,

How are you by now? I am doing ok. It came a big rain last night and it is still cloudy this morning. It is kind of cool here now.

Where is Odie Lee stationed now? Send him my address and tell him to write to me.

How long did Booley get to stay home? I haven't heard from any of the folks in two or three weeks. I went over to apply for a furlough and they told me that I would have to wait until I graduated before I applied. Then it would take three to four days for it to go through.

If I get a furlough, I may be broke and have to hike home.

We are getting ready to move over into a shipping squadron so that a new bunch of boys can move in here. I don't know if I will move with the rest or not. I signed the payroll with the permanent party men.

Well, I guess I will close since there is no news as usual. Write soon.

Love,
Odis

October 18, 1942

Dear Folks,

How are you by now? I am doing ok. We moved to a new area yesterday to let a new bunch into our area and we are really crowded. We have over 100 men in our barracks and we don't have any footlockers. I think all the guys are shipping out to Santa Monica, California Tuesday.

We have to go to school tomorrow night and then we graduate Tuesday morning. We have already had our final exams and I made 82 on mine.

It has really been raining up here for the last three or four days and it is pretty cold now.

I don't have any news so I will close. Write soon.

Love,
Odis

United States Army

Air Forces Technical Training Command

Be it known that

Private Clyde C. Primrose, Jr., 18115949,

Air Corps, Unassigned,

has satisfactorily completed the course for

Airplane Mechanics

as prescribed by the Air Forces Technical Training Command and Given at

Sheppard Field, Texas

In testimony whereof and by virtue of vested authority I

do confer upon him this

DIPLOMA

Given on this twentieth *day of* October

in the year of our Lord one thousand nine hundred and forty-two

COLONEL, AIR CORPS
COMMANDING

Odis after graduation.

October 20, 1942

Dear Folks,

How are you by now? I am ok, except I had to go to school until 12:00 last night and get up at 4:00 a.m. this morning. We got our diplomas this morning and my entire group is shipping out except one.

I have been so busy around here for the last few days that I haven't been over to see about the furlough yet. I am going over to check tomorrow.

Buck Mills went home last week and he was two hours late for school.

I got a letter from Westley today. He seems to be getting along o.k.

Bozo is shipping out today and I think he is going to California. His wife was up at the graduation exercise this morning.

It will probably be sometime next week before I get home if I do get a furlough. Write soon.

Love,
Odis

November 2, 1942

Dear Folks,

How are you by now? I am doing ok. I had to work yesterday. They don't have anymore Sundays here on Sheppard Field. There are some men off every day and they have school and drill on Sunday just the same.

I have been put on shipping orders at last. I just heard a rumor that we were going to Santa Ana, California and were going to live in a hotel while in training. I think that most enlisted pilots are put in pursuits now.

I haven't done a thing all day and I don't expect I will do much more tomorrow.

I got a letter form Bozo in Santa Monica, California and he is living in a hotel on the 6th floor.

I will close, I don't have any news. Write soon.

Love,
Odis

Odis had failed the cadet test twice, but continued with his application for enlisted pilot. He was approved by a board after passing his physical and receiving recommendation from people in his home town. He was sent to Kelly Field, Texas, on November 11, for his pre-flight training.

November 8, 1942

Dear Folks,

How are you by now? Fine I hope. I am doing fine I guess. I will be here three more days yet. I got a pass to go to town last night and went to a show. That's about all there is to do that doesn't cost a lot of money. I have really been lonesome without getting any mail from anybody.

I thought for awhile that I might be shipped to Santa Ana, California, but now I think I am going to Kelly. There was a bunch shipped out the other day to Memphis, Tenn.

I heard from Bozo the other day and he will service a P-38.

The boys from my barracks are going to school at the North American factory and they will service a B-25. Half of my squadron went to Seattle Washington to work on B-27s.

I went up and saw Buck Mills. He graduates a week from Tuesday.

It has been raining nearly every day for the last week, but it hasn't been very cold.

I am working in the orderly room today and I had to work K.P. Thursday. I mean it was rough. We had to work 16 hours and they would hardly let us stop all day long. I scrubbed floors nearly all day and washed greasy pots and pans the rest of the time.

I have run out of anything to write about so will close. Write soon.

Love,
Odis

P.S. I got the watch.

CHAPTER 4

Preflight Training

Odis arrived at Kelly Field in San Antonio, Texas on November 11, 1942, to begin pre-flight school. At that time, San Antonio was very much a military town. Fort Sam Houston, which was established in 1876, was there along with Kelly Field, Lackland (Part of Kelly until July, 1942), and Randolph Field. Kelly Field began as the original army air corps training center during WWI. San Antonio was also a very historic town, but Aviation Cadets had no time for sightseeing.

Pre-flight training lasted approximately nine weeks. The first two days were given in a fast pace of orientation, physicals, testing and screening. The cadet training was run on the underclassman and upperclassman system. The underclassmen were required to walk around with a rigid brace (A brace was to walk or sit at attention with your chin tucked down to your chest.), to sit on the front portion of their chairs while eating, and they could only address upperclassmen by saying, "Yes, Sir.", "No, Sir.", or "No excuse, Sir." This system of hazing was designed to instill ridged discipline and consistent reactions to situations. The upperclassmen could give demerits, better known as "gigs", for anything from not standing straight to a piece of thread on their uniform. The cadet had to walk in a square area for an hour for each "gig."

The actual training began after a few days consisting of physical training, marching, cleaning of barracks, guard duty, and K.P.

The cadet training consisted of long hours of classroom work in military subjects. Each phase of classroom work was followed by exams.

San Antonio Aviation Center
San Antonio, Texas
November 14, 1942

Dear Folks,

How are you doing by now? I am doing ok, I guess. I don't have time to write a letter, so I will just send you my address.

I arrived here November 11 and I mean it is tough. I will write you and tell you about it soon.

Love,
Odis

November 15, 1942

Dear Folks,

How are you? I am doing ok. I haven't received any gigs yet.

We are allowed six gigs a week and for each gig after six, we will have to walk a one hour tour at 130 steps a minute. The upperclassmen can give you a gig for any reason and can give as many as they want. One guy had to stand in a brace for awhile tonight because he passed a bowl with only six peas in it. After four and a half weeks, we lowerclassmen will become upperclassmen.

We have to snap to attention and say "Sir" to an upperclassman just as though he were an officer. We have to walk at attention at all times while out of the barracks and turn all corners square. We had to have our hair cut off. It could be no longer than 3/4 inch.

We have to wear sock supporters and have to buy our physical training equipment. I bought a pair of tennis shoes and I will have to get the rest of it payday. This is more like what you have heard about the army. It is strict. Every move you make has to be snappy. They blow the bugle every morning and we have to hit the floor before the echo dies away. We can't go to bed until 10:00 p.m. We have a study period from 8:15 p.m. until 9:30 p.m.

Well, I could go on writing rules and regulations of this place, but I will close. Answer soon.

Love,
Odis

November 23, 1942

Dear Folks,

How are you getting along by now? I am doing ok. so far. I received your letter today and was glad to hear from you. I haven't heard from any of the folks and have not written to anyone except Booley.

We have been on guard duty from seven last night until seven tonight, two hours on and four hours off. We didn't get very much sleep.

I won't get to come home for Christmas and I can't get off the post for about three more weeks.

I am glad you got another cow.

How long has daddy been gone off to work and what kind of work is he doing now? Do you still have the old car?

I have had an examination on math and on "ground forces", but I don't know what I made on either. We are taking aircraft identification now.

Well, I will close now and study awhile. Answer soon.

Love,
Odis

November 26, 1942

Dear Folks,

How are you doing by now? I am doing fine. We had today off except that we can't go anywhere. We really had a nice dinner. I have never seen a better meal prepared in my life. We had turkey, fruits, nuts, fruit salad, fruit cake and another kind of cake, ice cream, apple cider, English peas and any and everything you could think of to eat. They also gave everyone a package of cigarettes, a cigar and a box of candy.

I made 80 on my math examination. I hope I can do better on the next one.

We had a pressure chamber check yesterday. It was a big tank that they suck all the air out to give you a higher altitude pressure. It reduces the oxygen and you have trouble with your ears mostly. We were put in the chamber 18 at a time and gradually ran the pressure down to the pressure you would have at 18,000 feet. They held that pressure for seven minutes then we put on oxygen masks until we reached 30,000 ft. Then we took them off and the pressure was slowly lowered so that our ears would stop up or burst. One guy passed out on the second minute at 18,000 ft. They had to stop and go back up so that one or two could get their ears unstopped and then we would go back down some more. We finally got back to normal and got out in about an hour.

Have you heard from Booley lately? I wrote him but, I haven't heard from him yet. I got one letter from you and one from Grace Wiltshire since I have been here.

There should be a lot of people from Hemphill here. If you know any and can get their address, I might get a chance to look them up in two or three weeks when I get to go to town. Write soon.

Love,
Odis

November 27, 1942

Dear Dad,

How are you getting along by now? I received your letter today and was glad to hear from you. I also received a letter from mother today. I am glad Jack got a job. I know he will keep it if anybody with his experience could.

I am doing ok. I have taken only two exams so far and made 80 on math and 84 on ground forces. We are taking math, code and aircraft identification now.

(The remainder of this letter was not available.)

November 27, 1942

Dear Folks,

How are you by now? I hope Mary Jane gets ok. I am doing fine. I just got your letter a few minutes ago. I got a letter from daddy this morning.

I guess Jack is really happy over getting the job. I guess he will be afraid that daddy will want to tell him how to spend his money. I hope he doesn't spend what he is making now in proportion to the way he spent what little he did get. Maybe he can keep out of the hole.

Have you seen any of the folks lately? I sent Dixie and Guy a card to let them know where I am. What is R. T. doing these days? I guess he is still having trouble with his girls. Tell him to write me sometime.

I will be here until January 16 and there is a rumor that we will go to St. Louis, Mo. for primary training.

If you want to send me something for Christmas, don't send me anything to eat. I eat too much since I have been here. Write soon.

Love,
Odis

December 3, 1942

Dear Dad,

How are you by now? I am doing ok. I received your letter yesterday and sure was glad to hear from you. I haven't heard from mother in about a week.

I hope you can get a job at Beaumont. It will be closer to home and maybe the work won't be so hard. How is Jack getting along with his job? Do you think he will be able to hold it down?

I did guard duty last night and today and haven't had time to do anything. I took another physical examination day before yesterday and I passed everything, except that I have a murmur in my heart and I have to go to the hospital tomorrow for a recheck. The doctor said that I probably had the rickets when I was a kid and my chest was deformed. He said that other people have a chest like mine and it always caused the heart to make funny noises. If that is what it is, I will be ok.

I have gained a little weight since I have been here. I weigh 156 lbs. stripped now.

I got paid yesterday. I got $44.21 after laundry being taken out. I will go to Primary the 16th of January and I don't know when I will start getting flying pay.

Well, I will close. Write soon.

Love,
Odis

December 4, 1942

Dear Folks,

How are you by now? I am doing ok. I got a letter from daddy yesterday. I just received the first letter you wrote me to this place yesterday. I have not received the letter you said had a card in it. Send me Booley's address. I wrote him in El Paso. We had to do guard duty yesterday and the night before.

A letter just came in from you and I was glad to get it. I hope the kids get well and can keep well. I have an awful bad cold.

I am sending $15.00 this time, but next time if you can get along without it, I am going to buy me some clothes and a wrist watch.

I don't guess I will be sending many Christmas presents this year.

I will get to go to town some of these days and see what civilians look like. We are supposed to become upperclassmen the last of next week when these upperclassmen ship out.

Answer soon.

Love,
Odis

December 9, 1942

Dear Dad,

How are you by now? I am doing ok. I went to the hospital for a check on my heart and they hooked wires to my arms, legs and one over my heart and took some kind of test. From all accounts, they didn't find anything wrong because they turned me loose.

I got a letter from Pete Jones today and he is in Arkansas in the M.P. command.

Someone in our barracks here stole $40 about a week and half ago and got $20 more day before yesterday so we have been confined to the barracks ever since. We all had to put a blank envelope in a box yesterday so that the one that stole the money would have a chance to give it back. Today, we were sent into a room one by one with a blank envelope and the commanding officer said that he wasn't going to let the upperclassmen go to primary the last of this week unless he got the money back, so in one of the envelopes he got back $20 and they are threatening to wash out all 60 men in this barracks if they don't get the rest of the money. The upperclassmen were schedule to leave for primary Sunday. Quite a few of them had tears in their eyes because they might not be able to go and might be washed out as being under suspicion of theft.

Well, I will close. Write soon.

Love,
Odis

December 14, 1942

Dear Folks,

I am ok. except that I still have a cold. I received your letter today and am glad you are getting along ok. Tell Jack to write me a letter every now and then if he keeps working in Beaumont.

We haven't had any real bad weather down here. It has been pretty cold a few nights.

I got one letter from Dixie and she is the only one I have heard from. I have got letters from Bozo, Pete and Odie Lee. Bozo is in Hammer Field, California.

Well, I passed everything and at last I am an upperclassman and can sit on all of my chair while eating and we have quite a few advantages over the lowerclassmen. I am through with guard duty. Lowerclassmen pull all the guard duty.

The new lowerclassmen haven't arrived yet, but the commanding officer told the cadet officers that we were really gong to have to be tough on the lowerclassmen. All the lowerclassmen are allowed to say is, "Yes, Sir," "No, Sir," and "No excuse, Sir." If the lowerclassmen say anything back, we are to give them a few gigs. I only got 5 gigs the whole time I was a lowerclassman. One guy got 14 gigs yesterday. The upperclassmen are responsible for the lowerclassmen and if we don't get on the ball, we will get the gigs from the commanding officer.

Well, I will close for this time. Answer soon.

Love,
Odis

December 17, 1942

Dear Folks,

How are you getting along by now? I am ok. I received your card today and hated to hear that Jack is still sick. I am just about over my cold.

Well, today is the beginning of the last four and one-half weeks here and I mean we have a new and tougher schedule. Of course it is always tougher at first. We have to treat the lowerclassmen a lot rougher than we were treated when we came in. Half of them are half scared to death. Several of them resigned the first day. Some of the staff sergeants that came here don't want to take all this crap around here. We have them to where if an officer comes in they will holler, "Attention" so loud you can hear them a half mile away. We were all kept busy today. We had classes form 8:00 until 11:00 a.m. after cleaning the barracks and going to chow and then we ate and went to a lecture from 11:00 a.m. until 1:00 p.m. Then comes P.T. and then drill and a parade, then chow and it was 6:15 tonight when we got out of the mess hall and at 6:30 we fall out and drilled until 7:30.

We are taking physics now and it is really tough. All the classes have trouble with it. Men that have had college physics have trouble with it and there are about half of us who never had physics at all. We have 24 one-hour classes to learn it in. We are studying naval identification. We have 12 one-hour classes to learn 72 ships and to be able to tell the names and types when we see them. We had aircraft identification, but I already knew quite a few of those.

I am tired and sleepy, so I will close. I hope Jack gets better soon. Write soon.

Love,
Odis

December 19, 1942

Dear Folks,

How are you getting along by now? I hope Jack is still improving. I am doing ok. I received your letter today and was glad to hear from you.

They never did find out who stole the money here and they just dropped the whole thing. All of our group's upperclassmen were sent to Cuero for primary and they bought 14 quarts of whisky before they left and they all got drunk on the train. When they got down there, several of them were washed out. The cadet squadron commander was so drunk that he fell on his face in front of the major down there. The major picked him up and he fell on his face again and that was all for him.

I haven't heard from Booley, but I got a letter from Dixie about a week ago. I got a Christmas card from Mr. and Mrs. Walker today.

Well, I had better close and study my physics. We are going to have to go to school tomorrow just the same as any other day. Answer soon.

Love,
Odis

December 21, 1942

Dear Folks,

How are you getting along by now? Fine I hope. I have almost gotten over my cold. I received your letter this evening and am trying to answer it.

I have been studying physics and I mean I am snowed under. I can take six words a minute in code now and I think I can learn naval identification ok, but we have so many formulas that I can't learn them all. One problem was that a bomb hit the ground going 800 feet per second and it asked how high the plane was when it was dropped and what its acceleration was.

I received three Christmas cards today, one from Pete, Odie Lee and one from R. T.

Someone stole a cadet blouse out of our barracks today and I don't know whether we will get to go to town or not. We are supposed to get to go Wednesday, and Christmas Day is not supposed to be a day of duty.

Well, I hope you all have a merry Christmas and I hope Santa brings lots of stuff. I am sorry I could not send anything. I haven't had a chance to get out and buy anything even if I had the money. Answer soon.

Love,
Odis

P.S. I am sending a couple of pictures. They are not very good, but they are all I have.

Christmas Day
December 25, 1942

Dear Folks,

I just got your letter you mailed on the 23rd and I got a letter from Daddy yesterday. I hope you all can keep well and Jack can keep improving. I have just about cleared my cold up.

We don't have a thing to do today. I haven't made my bed up yet and we just got back from dinner. We had an even better meal than we had Thanksgiving. We had better, more and a bigger variety of food than can be bought by civilians.

We had open post Wednesday and we went to town. It's a pretty nice place, but anything you do or buy costs you plenty of money. One of the biggest hotels right in the middle of town is run by the cadets. No other soldiers are allowed in. I spent the day looking the town over. We had our first physics test yesterday and I made 81 and I was really proud.

I haven't heard from Booley. I would like to know where he is.

I received the diary and I want to thank Jack for it. I hope by the next Christmas I will get each and everyone of you a present.

The only worry I have now is to study and keep on the ball and get through the flying training. I am just beginning it now. The biggest percent wash out for disorderly conduct, absent without leave and I am going to make sure that nothing washes me out. If I get sick flying or something like that will be the only thing that will wash me out.

I will close. Write soon.

Love,
Odis

January 3, 1943

Dear Folks,

I received your letters but have been so busy I haven't had time to answer them and I haven't got time to write much tonight.

I am getting along ok. I weigh 164 lbs. now. Another guy and I are going to run the 100 yard dash for our squadron in a wing track meet.

We will be through with all of our school classes on the 10th and leave for primary about the 14th.

We have had really a lot of good weather. It has not been cold enough to frost since I have been here.

I haven't heard from any of the folks at Pineland and I haven't heard from Dixie but once. I will have to close the lights will go out in a minute. I will try to write more next time. Answer soon.

Lots of love,
Odis

January 7, 1943

Dear Folks,

How are you getting along by now? I am doing fine. We had our final examinations for pre-flight school today and I have passed everything now. We only have to take 8 words a minute in code and 3 words a minute in blinker and I passed that about a week ago.

We have open post tomorrow, but I'm not going to town. We won't have anymore classes here, but we will have physical training and a few lectures. They are always sure that we are kept busy.

We will start flying the second day after we get to primary and we will fly about 60 hours the weeks we are there.

I got a letter from Odie Lee and he told me about being home. I got a letter from Pete and he said he might get to go home soon.

Where is C. B. Taylor now?

It seems funny not to have anything to study. I guess I will catch up on my sleep.

I'll close until next time. Answer soon.

Lots of love,
Odis

January 13, 1943

Dear Folks,

How are you getting along by now? I am doing ok. I was in a medley relay team at the track meet for wing championship and we won. We are going to run for post championship this evening. I ran one 220 yards in it.

We are shipping our baggage out in the morning and we are leaving day after tomorrow for Cuero, Texas. That is about 90 miles east of here. It will be a little closer home than here.

Well, I hope you all keep well and I will write as soon as I arrive at Cuero. Until next time.

Love,
Odis

CHAPTER 5

Primary Flight Training

Aviation cadets completing preflight training at Kelly Field were sent to training sites primarily in Texas under the Gulf Coast Training Command. Odis was sent to Cuero, Texas. The name Cuero comes from a Spanish name meaning Rawhide and is located in South Texas, 90 miles Southeast of San Antonio, and approximately 60 miles inland from the Gulf of Mexico. The area was flat with bountiful agriculture production.

The proximity to the Gulf created severe weather conditions of rain, wind, fog, and overcast skies during January thru late March of 1943. Not having suitable weather, flight instructions were many times delayed or cancelled, adding even more pressure on the men to complete the required number of flying hours in the specified amount of time.

Odis arrived at Cuero on January 15, 1943, to begin Class 43G. The training facility was operated by a civilian operation named Brayton Flying Service. The facility was staffed by civilian instructors, along with a small number of army personnel and mechanics.

The flight training was in a Fairchild PT-19A "Cornell", which was a two-seater with an open cockpit. The plane was powered with a 175HP Ranger L-440 engine with a top speed of 124MPH and a maximum ceiling of 16,000 feet. The instructor sat in the front seat and the cadet in the rear seat. This was the first time most of the cadets had flown in an airplane. Very few of them even knew how to drive a car. Many of them were from farms and did have experience behind a horse or on a tractor.

Primary training as well, worked on the cadet system of underclassmen and upperclassmen, and continued to instill discipline. Due to the need for pilots, reduced training was from ten weeks down to nine by January, 1943. The training consisted of ground school training on aircraft recognition, navigation, radio operation, aircraft equipment, principles of flight, and link training. The hands-on flight training consisted of flying patterns, stalls, spins, acrobatics, forced landing, and cross country flights. From 40%-50% were of cadets washed out for lack of ability or failure to follow instructions.

Brayton Flying Service
Cuero, Texas
January 16, 1943

Dear Folks,

I arrived here yesterday and was issued flying equipment and this morning we had an inspection and a lecture. This afternoon we are going out on the line and meet our instructors and get acquainted with the airplanes.

We have real nice beds with springs under them and the food is the best. The country around here is a little different from that at San Antonio. There are quite a few scrubby holly and bushes down here. This is a small place and there are only about 350 cadets here and the mechanics and instructors are civilian. Civilian instructors are always rougher than army instructors.

Well, I will close. Answer soon.

Love,
Odis

Sunday
January 17, 1943

Dear Jack,

How's every little thing by now? I hope you haven't gotten sick again. I hope you can get to work as much as you can. We are having some pretty rough weather down here at Cuero. The upper class did not get to fly any today and they are way behind with their flying. If the weather clears up I will start flying tomorrow afternoon. We have to get in 60 hours of flying in nine weeks we are here, regardless of the weather.

There are only about 350 cadets here in this school and they have civilian mechanics and instructors. The barracks are one story buildings with concrete floors and varnished walls and we have beds with springs just like home. We have civilian cooks and the food is the best that can be had.

We were issued leather flying suits that are fur lined and big fur lined boots that fit over your shoes. The helmets are leather and fur lined. We have to wear our goggles around our neck everywhere we go until we solo.

Tell S. T. that I will write them later on. I don't have time now. Answer soon.

Love,
Odis

Odis in sheep skin flight suit.

Tuesday
January 19, 1943

Dear Folks,

How are you by now? I am doing ok. I guess. It has really been cold down here the last two days.

I went up for 51 minutes yesterday and 50 minutes today. I got sick both times and I mean I don't like it a bit. I threw up all over the plane today. I think I would like it if I wouldn't get sick, but I haven't seen anything thrilling about flying yet.

Well, I don't have any news so I will close until I hear from you.

Love,
Odis

It is common for pilot trainees to get sick during the first phase of flight training. This is expected and does not disqualify a cadet if he overcomes getting sick after several flights.

Thursday
January 21, 1943

Dear Folks,

How are you getting along by now? I received your letter today and I also got one from Jack.

I have been flying everyday, but I don't like it a bit better than I did. I have been sick ever since I have been here. I have lost about ten pounds weight since I came down here. I am going to try to stick it out and get through here some how. Everyone says that I will like it later on.

I hope you can stay well. Answer soon.

Love,
Odis

Thursday
January 21, 1943

Dear Folks,

How are you getting along by now? I'm not doing so well. I have been just about sick ever since I have been here. I haven't got to where I like this flying yet. We did spins and stalls and everything today. There are a million things to remember in flying.

Our barracks didn't pass inspection and we can't go to town the first open post.

Well, I will close and write more next time. Answer soon.

Love,
Odis

Sunday
January 24, 1943

Dear Folks,

How are you getting along by now? I am doing ok. I went up five times last week and got three hours and 55 minutes flying time in. I didn't get so very sick the last times I went up.

The brakes you get here count a lot. I got a good instructor and with a little luck, I will make it through here. I guess I will learn to like it later on. We only have two classes a day, one is navigation and the other is airplanes.

I will be flying in the mornings this week and it is usually foggy and you can't fly, so I might not get in too much flying this week.

I got a letter from Bozo. He is stationed in Muroc, California.

I will write more next time. Answer soon.

Love,
Odis

Tuesday
January 26, 1943

Dear Folks,

How are you getting along by now? I received all your letters today and was glad to get them. I hope you all can stay well. I have a cold, but it is a mild one. We have had some mighty bad weather. There wasn't any flying done yesterday.

I had a bad day today. I was the last of us three to go up this morning and it was really cold. Our instructor cussed all morning until he got to me and he was wound up right. We went up and he kept getting madder and madder and cussing louder and louder and brought me back in 20 minutes. I always dread for my time to come to go up. They cuss and fuss at you so that you don't know what you are doing. My instructor is not the only one that cusses and raises cane. They all do it. I get so disgusted I can hardly stand it sometimes. It doesn't make me any difference whether I wash out or not. If you don't keep your bunk and wall locker just so all week, you are kept in camp and can't go to town.

I will close this time and hope I have something better to write about next time. Answer soon.

Love,
Odis

Monday
February 1, 1943

Dear Folks,

How are you getting along by now? I am ok. I received your letter today that you mailed on the 30th.

I did not get to fly Saturday and we haven't started flying Sundays yet. It was awfully cloudy this morning the ceiling was about 1000 feet, but I did S turns and the rest of the time we were shooting landings and take offs. I guess I will solo sometime this week. Four or five of the boys soloed today and were walking around this evening with their clothes on backwards. You have to get someone to button your clothes up in the back for you. You can quit wearing your goggles around your neck after you solo.

Well, it will be some time after July before I get a furlough or even a three day pass if I don't wash out before then.

I hope you can all stay well and up able to go. I have a bad cold, but I'm still on the go. I am scheduled to fly first in the morning. I will take off just at daybreak.

I have had a few Kodak pictures made but haven't sent the film off yet, but when I get them back I will send them to you. I had one made where I was standing by one of the planes with my parachute on.

Well, I don't have anything to write about so I will close. Answer soon.

Love
Odis

Saturday
February 6, 1943

Dear Folks,

How are you getting along by now? I am in the hospital now. I got hit over the kidney this morning playing football. I think I will be out Monday so I can fly. I didn't get to fly today and it was the first real pretty day we have had. I didn't fly but two days this week. I haven't soloed yet. Over half of the boys have soloed, but they were flying in the afternoon this week and got more time in. They washed out one from our barrack today and some barracks they have washed out four or five already. They wash out some men after they get 40 hours in.

One boy stalled out about 30 feet from the ground when coming in for a landing. He dropped in and broke a main spar on one wing and cracked one landing gear. I saw one fellow ground loop on his solo. There's hardly any way to get hurt in these ships. One boy tore the landing gear off his plane and only got a broken nose. Of course, out of so many men, there are going to be a few accidents. I knew one boy that was killed up at Sweet Water. He put it in a spin at about 4000 feet and didn't pull it out until it got to 2000 feet. He started spinning the opposite way and kept spinning until he hit the ground, his instructor and all. There has been three instructors and two students killed at Sweet Water, Texas in the last week.

My instructor's youngest brother is reported among the missing. The last they heard from him he was on a navy tanker that was sunk.

Well, I will close. Answer soon.

Love,
Odis

P.S. I am inclosing some pictures. They are not very good. I sent Grace two of the best ones I had.

Saturday
February 6, 1943

Dear Bud, (He called his brother Jack, Bud sometimes.)

How are you by now? I am doing ok. I have only been up twice this week. We are having some awfully bad flying weather. It is either foggy or the clouds are too low every morning. I am going to start flying in the afternoons next week. I am getting to where I like to fly a lot better.

We had an AT-6 land here one night last week with its landing gear up and it bent the propeller up and that was about all it hurt. We are flying the PT-19 plane here. It has 175HP Ranger engines in Fairfield planes. They are the latest primary trainers out.

I got a letter from Grace today. She said that she was in Beaumont the other day. She said that Merline wanted my address, but I don't much care if she never gets my address. Grace said that Pete made Corporal.

If you ever want to call me, just call collect to (9529) telephone number in my barracks in Brayton Flying Service. I think I am going to Houston this weekend.

Well, I don't have any news, so I will close. Answer soon.

Love,
Odis

Monday night
February 8, 1943

Dear Folks,

How are you by now? I feel ok, but am still in the hospital. They have not told me anything other than I can get out when my kidneys get alright.

It has been fair and sunshiny the last three days, but some of the boys came in to see me tonight. They said it was so windy that they couldn't fly today. I don't think I will get sick any more under ordinary circumstances. When we get to acrobatics I might get sick.

All these things about wearing your goggles around your neck until you solo and wearing your clothes backwards the day you solo is just tradition. You don't know what day you are going to solo, but if you solo, you can come back and wear all your clothes backward the rest of the day.

Well, I spent the whole day in the hospital and it was my birthday. I don't feel a bit older. I am still about the youngest in this school.

We have a final coming up in navigation tomorrow, but I don't think it will be so hard. I have had three major exams so far and I made 88, 90 and 95 on them. On "Theory of Flight," I made 92 and 96.

Well, I will close. I am a little nervous tonight and can hardly write. Hope you can read this. Answer soon.

Love,

Odis

Thursday
February 11, 1943

Dear Folks,

How are you by now? I am ok and out of the hospital. It was so windy yesterday we could hardly fly. I was only up 30 minutes. Today it was still and I soloed. I didn't do so good, but I got the ship back safe. The first time I went up I flew the pattern three times before I finally let it stay on the ground. The next time I went around four times. I would hit the ground and bounce and I would give the gun and take off.

I got your letter today and one from Jack yesterday.

There are boys washing out every day. They have already got 3 out of my barracks and 8 & 10 out of the other barracks. They are washing out boys here in the upper class with 40 to 50 hours flying time. Above 40% of the upper class have already washed out.

I hope Jack can come down and see me. I will probably have to fly every day after this week because I am behind now, but we are having good weather so I will catch up.

I hope you all can stay up and well and I will try to write as often as I can. Answer soon.

Love,
Odis

Thursday
February 11, 1943

Dear Jack,

How are you by now? I am doing fine and am out of the hospital.

I soloed today. That's one little hump that I have made. If I can keep going, with luck I may get through this place. I have 10 hours & 15 minutes flying time now. I am a little behind schedule.

Well, if they ever send you to Tyler for an examination you will practically be in the army. They don't turn anybody down these days. I hate to see you have to go to the army because a fellow that is not absolutely in perfect physical condition is held back in every way. If you do get into anything, try the air corps because you don't have so much physical training.

All this heroism and exciting advertisement they give the marines, there is not a thing to it. They give cadets and pilots a lot of advertisement, but it is not a bit thrilling like they build it up to be. Any pilot will tell you he wouldn't go through with all the stuff you have to if he had it to do again. It's worth plenty of money to be a flyer, but it is plenty of work to it. Lots of boys say they would like to fly. There is not a man here that gets a thrill out of his flying. I am going to give it all I got and make a good pilot, because there's nothing better if you can make it.

Well, I will close. Answer soon.

Love,
Odis

Sunday
February 14, 1943

Dear Folks,

How are you by now? I received your letter yesterday and was glad to hear from you. I am glad you are getting along ok.

We had to fly this morning from 8:00 until 1:00 this evening. I have been doing pretty good flying since I got out of the hospital. Thursday I made five landings solo and I finally made a good one and also made good ones on Friday and Saturday. I have passed my supervised solos and today I was shooting stages. Each stage consists of seven solo trips around the pattern on the field. I completed one stage today and I hope I can complete another tomorrow. We have to shoot two stages before we can clear the area. After we clear the area, we can check out a plane everyday and take it up solo for an hour. I flew out of the pattern and flew around for about 10 minutes and then came in. My instructor just wanted to see if I could come in on the pattern when he was not with me. I came in and made every turn just right and made a good three point landing and he said it was ok. The boys that are left in the upper class are leaving for basic at Waco tomorrow or the next day.

I have only been to town one time since I have been here and it doesn't look like we are going to get another open post.

Well, I don't have any news, so I will close. Answer soon.

Love,
Odis

Tuesday
February 16, 1943

Dear Jack,

How are you by now? I am doing ok. I received your letter today and was glad to hear from you. I hope you can get along good with your job.

I have been doing pretty good flying the last week. I soloed and shot about 20 landings and I have got to where I can land without a bit of trouble. I get to take a ship out tomorrow for an hour to practice. It makes me feel good when you hear them say, "Student Primrose, take out number 56 out for an hour" and I get to go get it and take it off for an hour. My instructor has five students and I think he is going to wash out one. We will start acrobatics when we get about 30 hours flying time in.

I will be glad for you to come down and see me. I will be here for four and a half more weeks if I don't wash out. We had to fly last Sunday and we may have to fly every Sunday from now on. I will let you know in a week or so when to come.

I am sending a picture or two that I have. When you go home, you can see the others.

Well, I will close. Answer soon.

Love,
Odis

Wednesday
February 17, 1943

Dear Folks,

How are you doing? I am doing ok. I received your letter today with the questions in it and I will try to answer them. AV/S is Aviation Student and AV/C is Aviation Cadet. If I get my wings, I will be a flight officer which gets the same pay as a Second Lieutenant and rates a salute from the enlisted men. Instead of a gold bar, I will wear a gold bar with a blue strip down the center. Ten percent of the cadets get second Lieutenant and the rest get flight officer same as the AV/S. If you ever wash out of flying you will never get another chance.

It was cloudy and foggy this morning and we didn't get to fly until about 11:00. I got a solo ship and went out for an hour. I went up through the scattered clouds and did three or four stalls and then I came down and did some S turns and 8's then came in the pattern just right and made a good landing. The pattern and landing is easy once you get use to putting your flaps down and setting down wind legs and base leg down right. You have to cut your engine at the right time and then bring it in and stall it out about a foot above the ground and let it drop in. One boy dropped in about 20 feet the other day and broke a center section.

The reason you get washed out here is for flying, generally. They have been checking stalls, spins, practiced forced landings, landings flying in and out of the pattern and keeping altitude in turns and in straight and level flight. Keeping a ship at 500 feet while doing S turns and making corrections for the wind at the same time is hard to do. They will cut the engine and holler "Forced landing" and you have to find a field right quick and go through a certain procedure in getting the plane into it. We will all get a 20 hour check. I could name a lot of other things, but I know I couldn't tell it in a way you could understand. Flying for the army has to be a certain way and precision flying altogether.

Well, I guess I have written enough. Answer soon.

Love,
Odis

Odis was explaining that an AV/C was a cadet with two years of college, or who scored high on the Aviation Cadet test. Both the AV/C and the AV/S received the same training and would have the same responsibilities, but the AV/C would be commissioned as a 2nd Lieutenant while the AV/S would be commissioned as a Flight Officer. (This was an unfair system, and was later changed so that all pilots were commissioned as 2nd Lieutenants.) The pilot of any aircraft was in command of the aircraft even if the co-pilot out ranked him. If the Flight Officer was the pilot, the co-pilot would be under his command even if he was a 2nd Lieutenant or a 1st Lieutenant.

Tuesday
February 23, 1943

Dear Folks,

How are you by now? I am ok.

We have been flying the last two days, but it has been pretty rough air.

I have 24 hours in now and I get a school or army check ride tomorrow or the next day. It is not elimination check, but if I fail it my next one will be an elimination check ride. My check pilot will be "One way O'Keef," an army captain. He checked eight the other day and one passed. Out of the thirty men in my barracks, they shipped four out Monday and already two more have washed out. By next Monday, they will have quite a few more of us. If you are lucky and have a good day when you have your check rides you will be ok, but some days you get started off wrong and can't think like you can others.

I got a letter from one of the boys that I went through A.M. school with and he is in South Carolina where the biggest majority of my class is. One boy that slept right across from me got killed in a B-25 crash the 6th of January and another one of the boys fell off a wing and fractured an elbow. The most of the boys are corporals and sergeants now. One of the boys went to gunning school in Las Vegas and he is a Staff Sergeant. He is in Topeka, Kansas now. One of the boys has already been shipped across. Three or four of the boys are in Utah, three or four are in Florida and three are in Atlantic City.

I don't have any news, so will close. Answer soon.

Love,
Odis

Friday
February 27, 1943

Dear Jack,

How are you by now? I am doing ok. I got your letter yesterday and will try to answer it as we are not flying this afternoon because the wind is so bad. I have 27 hours flying time in although I am several hours behind. My whole section is behind. When I get 30 hours in I will start flying in the front seat. I will be able to do spins and acrobatics when I am up solo. I had a check ride yesterday, but I was only up 20 minutes and all I got to do was my stalls. The captain said the ride was satisfactory, but that he would have to ride with me again in a day or two. I will also get a school check in a day or two. The main thing wrong with taking check rides is that I get nervous and can't fly natural.

We get to go to town every Wednesday night now if we don't get restricted for anything. If you come down, come on a weekend. If we fly Sunday, we get a pass on Saturday night from 7:00 until 10:00 at night. I don't know whether you can get a pass to come on the field or not.

Well, I don't have any news, so I will have to close. Let me know when you are coming down and if I wash out I will let you know. Answer soon.

Love,
Odis

Tuesday
March 2, 1943

Dear Folks,

How are you by now? I am doing ok. It is raining this morning. I don't know whether we will ever catch up with this flying or not. We are getting further behind all the time. I flew two hours and forty minutes yesterday, but I was up when I was supposed to be in Link Training and I got 10 gigs and that means I will have to walk 6 hours next Sunday evening in front of the orderly room.

I got in the front seat yesterday. It is just like learning flying again. I shot 180degrees overhead approach stage in the front seat solo. I am checked out in spins, stalls and lazy eights and I am practicing slow rolls and snap rolls dual. Yesterday I was first to go up with my instructor and we went up above the clouds which were practically solid and the sun was shining on the top of the clouds and there was no fog. It was really pretty. We only go up about 6000 ft. in these PTs and do most of our work at about 3000 feet and stunts at 500 feet.

An AT-6A crashed on our field Saturday night while we were in town and it blew up when it hit the ground. They cleaned it up and we never knew what happened.

I got a letter from Jack and he said he might get to come see me. I will have very little time off. If we fly on Sunday we only get off Saturday night from 7 until 10. I am going to see if he could get a pass to come on the field. He said he wanted to see me fly.

Well, I will have to quit and go to the shop to get some instruction on 50 hour inspection. What I learned at Sheppard Field has helped me a lot since I have been here. Answer soon.

Love,
Odis

Monday
March 8, 1943

Dear Folks,

How are you by now? I received your letter Saturday, but I have been pretty sick the last week and still trying to stay out of the hospital. It looks like I will have to go on sick call tomorrow morning. I went up for 55 minutes solo this evening and got to feeling so bad that I came back to the barracks. We have been having bad weather down here. We only flew two days last week. We had to fly yesterday.

You had better keep Jack working in Beaumont if it will keep him out of the army. I am pretty sure he will pass physically. I have noticed that the men coming in the army here lately are shipped across from 4 to 6 months and theres not many men across that were not in the army before the war started. These boys from 18 to 21 will be doing the fighting pretty soon. One fellow here in my barracks, who has been in the army for 4 years, has a brother who was in for five months and was sent across, but he is still here.

I got a letter from the boy in Carolina and he said that it wouldn't be long before all of my bunch from Sheppard Field would be across. They are all in combat units.

Well, I don't have any news, so I will close. Answer soon.

Love,
Odis

Thursday
March 11, 1943

Dear Folks,

How are you by now? I am in the hospital, but am not very sick. I don't know when I will get out. I am pretty sure to be set back in class. I got your letter Tuesday, the first day I was in here.

I hope Faye is getting over her whooping cough by now and that the baby has got rid of the bad cold.

Well, I haven't done any walking yet. It seems that the records or something got lost, but I guess they will catch up with me yet. I am hoping they forgot to give the gigs to me.

Well, it is cloudy again today and the boys aren't flying. The afternoon shift got to fly yesterday.

I don't worry about me being in the hospital. I only had 99.4 fever and they put me to bed. I have some boy's radio and I have music, news and everything all day and most of the night. He is on furlough. They are giving me cod liver oil starting today, so I guess I will have to get well and get out. Answer soon.

Love,
Odis

Friday
March 12, 1943

Dear Folks,

How are you by now? One of the boys just brought a letter from you to me. I am still in the hospital. I don't know when I will get out. I am still taking cod liver oil regularly.

We had a big shower late this evening and the wind has been blowing so hard they couldn't fly all day. Most of the boys have from 40 to 50 hours and are supposed to leave the 20th. They are all sweating check rides and trying to get enough hours to go to basic. The maximum time permissible per day is 2 and 1/2hours. We were figuring up tonight out of the 27 men who was in who were in B flight at preflight and came down here, 9 have already washed out and the other 18 of us have from 24 to 10 hours to go.

You asked in one of your letters when I would get my wings. Well, if everything from now on goes off smooth I will get my wings in about 6 months. I will be here another 4 and 1/2 weeks, at basic for 9 weeks and then to advanced for 9 weeks then get my wings in September. This is a solid 9 month grind course.

To be an officer you can go to O.C.S. for three months and come out a Second Lieutenant.

Pete Jones thinks he will stay in Arkansas for the duration.

Well, I hope all can get well and keep well. Answer soon.

Love,
Odis

Monday
March 15, 1943

Dear Folks,

How are you by now? I am out of the hospital, but am still grounded. My instructor put one boy up for elimination after he had 45 hours in and I am afraid to go back to flying now. He told some of the boys that if I got back on the flying line the first of this week that I would be washed out within two days because I was so far behind. I am going to tell the doctor to do anything to keep me grounded the rest of this week and then I will be helt over with the next class. I will have it easy if I am held over. I wont have any ground school or Link Trainer. All I will have to do is flying and I will be about 20 hours ahead of that class. My instructor gets a new bunch of students next time, but he is going to try to carry me over. I don't care if I get a new instructor. The one I got just cusses all the time whether we do good or bad.

One of the boys and his instructor was doing a practice forced landing and when they got down as low as they wanted to get they gave it the gun and it went dead just after they got out of the field about 200 feet high and landed in a mesquite patch and tore the plane all to pieces, but neither one got a scratch. As long as you keep your head you won't get hurt in these PTs.

My class is just now learning loops, snap rolls and slow rolls good enough to do them solo and I mean they are really cutting up. You see as many planes flying upside down as right side up.

Well, I don't have anything else to write so I will close. Answer soon.

Love,
Odis

Saturday
March 20, 1943

Dear Folks,

How are you by now? Fine I hope. I am ok, but haven't been flying any since I got out of the hospital. All the boys left for basic at Waco this morning. I sure wish I could have gone with them. Another class will come in tomorrow.

I have 36 hours in and I am transferred back with 43 men who have only 12 hours. If I haven't forgotten how to fly since I went into the hospital I think I will make it. After you get in Basic they don't wash out but 4% and your chances of getting your wings are good. I am pretty sure I will be sent to Waco if I get through here.

Well, I guess all those chickens will be dead with old age before I get home. If I ever get basic or advanced and am close enough, I will come to Hemphill and give you a buzz. On those AT-6A's you can put the propeller in low pitch and nearly knock the window pains out they are so loud. We have some of the boys in basic and advanced to come back here and fly in formation just above the row of hangars. There is an advance school at Victoria about 30 miles from here. One of our boys tore up another ship the other day. He tore the wings, landing gear off and turned it upside down. He only got a few scratches.

I have no other news. Answer soon.

Love,
Odis

Wednesday
March 24, 1943

Dear Folks,

How are you by now? I am doing ok. I received your letter today and was glad to hear from you. I got a letter from Jack and he wanted to know why I had not written him. I didn't even know he was back in Beaumont. I also got a letter from Guy.

Well, I flew Sunday and Monday, but the weather has been too bad the last two days. I have a new instructor and he doesn't cuss quite so much. You don't have to worry about these crashes. The percentage is very low. We have about 150 planes here and on flying days they are in the air about 5 hours each and there hasn't been anyone killed so far. There were 4 A Ts that crashed right around here awhile back and killed 8 men, but they just got too close to the ground at night. It was their own fault. Fifty percent of all accidents could be avoided.

Well, I guess I will have to close and write Jack a line or two. Answer soon.

Love,
Odis

Wednesday
March 24, 1943

Dear Jack,

How are you by now? Ok, I hope. I received your letter today or card it was. I am doing ok. I got to fly Sunday and Monday, but the weather has been too bad the last two days. I got a letter from Guy and one from home today.

Is William working there in Beaumont now? Do you have Jessie Jr.'s address? I would like to write him.

When do you think you could come down to see me? About the best time I could think of would be about a week from next Sunday. If I have to fly on Sunday, I think I could get you a pass to come on the post and you could watch us fly. Maybe I won't be washed out by then. I am going to give them hell before I wash out.

Well, I don't have a thing to write about. I have not written Grace in about two weeks and I got a letter from her and she said she just loved airplanes and she kind of liked me. I never did tell her I liked her and that's the first time she ever wrote anything like that.

When Merline went to Beaumont I quit writing her and one day I got a letter from her and she was raising hell. She said if I didn't want to write to her she did not give a dam. She said just go ahead and spend my time writing Grace. It was funny to me because I didn't give a shit whether she wrote to me or not. I don't guess I could ever make myself like her, but I wrote back and told her I was sorry and explained a little just to see what she would write back. The next letter she said she wasn't going to send me one of her pictures because she guessed that I had too many Hemphill girls' pictures already. I want you to write me and tell me who Grace and Merline are going with. I'm going to fix Merline up some of these days and Grace will try to give me a line, but I am going to be prepared. Odie Lee wrote me two letters after he got back off his furlough and all he could talk about was his little dumbbell and I see what happened to him.

Answer soon.

Love,
Odis

Thursday
April 1, 1943

Dear Jack,

I got your letter the other day and was glad to hear from you.

I had a check ride the other day and it was unsatisfactory, so I may not be here in two more weeks, but I will know in time to let you know whether to come down or not. All you will have to do to get in touch with me after you get into Cuero is to call me at Brayton F. S. or come out to the airport and they will get me down to the gate. Well, I don't have any news so will close. Answer soon.

Love,
Odis

Thursday
April 1, 1943

Dear Folks,

How are you by now? I received your letter yesterday and was glad to hear from you. I hope the measles won't hurt Shirley and the kids much.

I have been flying a little every day. I am flying in the mornings this week and we have a fog until about 10:00. I have more time than anyone else and I have to wait until last to get a solo ship.

I had a check ride with the director of flying here and I got an unsatisfactory on it. I am hoping I don't wash out after getting this far.

Well, I don't have any news so will close. Answer soon.

Love,
Odis

Sunday night
April 4, 1943

Dear Folks,

How are you by now? I am doing ok. I received your letter the other day and was glad to hear from you. I sent you a $40 money order. I hope you got it ok.

I flew three hours yesterday and I had a check ride included and I passed it. I have a better chance of getting through here now. I have 50:15 hours.

I was walking tours this evening and Jack came down to the gate and I got to quit for the day. He is coming out tomorrow evening to watch us fly. I hope I don't get a check ride and wash out while he is here.

Well I got to go to town last night for the first time in two weeks although there was not anything to do but go to a show or get drunk.

It has finally quit being bad weather and the last two or three days it has been really hot. We start wearing khakis tomorrow.

Answer soon.

Love,
Odis

Tuesday
4-6-43

Dear Folks,

I received your letters yesterday and was glad to hear from you. I am doing ok. I have not had anymore check rides. Jack came out and stayed all evening. I think he got a kick out of watching them take off and land. I didn't go up but once and I was solo then. It looks as though we are going to have a pretty day today.

There is never anything to write about around here, so I will close. Answer soon.

Love,
Odis

Sunday night
April 11, 1943

Dear Folks,

How are you by now? I had one check ride since Jack was here and passed it, but I still have one more army check ride. I only lack four more hours. I went over today and sat around all evening and they never did give me a ship.

I got a little scare the other day. My engine quit and I began to look for a field to land in. I switched gas tanks and worked the wobble pump and got it started. I had run one tank dry. One boy ran through three barbed wire fences, hit and killed a cow and tore the ship up, but it did not hurt him.

It is getting to be real summer time down here. It has been pretty cloudy, but we have been flying right on.

I will try to write more next time. Answer soon.

Love,
Odis

P. S. Don't send me any money yet, but I may need about $15.00 a little later on.

Thursday night
April 15, 1943

Dear Folks,

How are you by now? I received your letter today. I am doing ok and I have 61 hours and just lack one. I have been on two cross country flights and have one tomorrow. I am going to Hallettsville on to Gonzales and back to Cuero, about a hundred mile trip. We have our map strapped on our knee and the course drawn out. We had two boys to get lost and ended at Victoria. We carry four flying hours of gasoline and the cross country only takes an hour.

My instructor left this evening and I guess all his students will finish tomorrow.

I hope you can come out to see me when I get to Waco. I imagine the best time to come would be sometime during the last part of the course there. We leave here next Thursday and if you send me the $15.00 right away I will get it before I leave. Don't send a money order, just send the money. I will get it ok. I won't get to come home any time soon. I thought maybe I would get a three day pass, but I can't.

Well there is no news except they washed out a couple of boys for hedgehopping the other day. One boy hung a piece of highline on his tail wheel and landed on an auxiliary field and took it off and he did not get caught.

Well, I will close. Answer soon.

Love,
Odis

303rd AAF FLYING TRAINING DETACHMENT

Brayton

FLYING SERVICE

CUERO, TEXAS

This is to certify that [illegible]
of the class of [illegible] *has satisfactorily completed*
the prescribed course of elementary pilot training
and ground school, and is hereby awarded
this diploma this Twenty second *day of* April
Nineteen Hundred and Forty three

Commanding
303rd AAF Flying Training Detachment

President
Brayton Flying Service

CHAPTER 6

Basic Flight Training

Odis arrived at Waco Army Air Field on Saturday, April 24, 1943 for Class 43-H. Waco was a medium size city located on the Brazos River in the black land country of Central Texas. All of those who had completed primary training in Cuero were sent for basic training to Waco. When he caught up with his original class, he learned that the wash out rate had been 50 percent. This was an indication of how difficult the primary training had been. The small number of letters he wrote during his basic flight training is a sign of how difficult and time consuming this phase was.

Basic flight training was similar to primary, but more detailed. The cadet system was still the same with physical training and barracks inspections, etc. Basic added longer cross country flights, formation flying, instrument flying, and night flying. The biggest change was in the size, power, and speed of the planes.

The Vultee BT-13B "Valiant" was a 4,227 lb plane with 450 HP Pratt & Whitney engine, having a maximum speed of 155 mph. The cab was enclosed with seats for the instructor and one or two students. The student pilots now had to use two-way radio equipment with ground control, operate landing flaps, and use a two-position variable pitch propeller.

After successfully completing basic flight, the cadets would be sent to the next stage of flight training. Depending upon the military requirements and recommendations by instructors, they would be sent to multi engine or fighter pilot training.

Waco Army Air Field
Waco, Texas
Sunday
April 25, 1943

Dear Folks,

How are you getting along by now? I haven't been here long enough to find out how I'm going to like it. We didn't leave on Thursday as we planned. They couldn't get transportation then, but we left Cuero at 1:00p.m. Friday and arrived at Waco at 6:00 Saturday morning. We had lectures yesterday and today on rules and regulations. We fly tomorrow morning.

I arrived here to my disappointment to find that about half the boys that were in my barracks in Cuero had washed out. However, the percentage is pretty low here. The main trouble seems to be to solo this ship. It's a big jump from a 175 HP to a 450. The casualties are low here because they won't let a fellow solo unless they know he can fly. The ground school is pretty tough here too. If your grades are below 75 in any subject, you don't get to go to town and have to attend night classes. Some boys never get to go to town.

All of us students are supposed to eat in the army mess halls, but this post is on field rations and the food is terrible so we all signed to eat at the cadet mess hall although it will cost $12.00 a month. In Cuero we were on detached service and we saved about $17.00 a month. We get good food at the cadet mess and I am satisfied.

Well, I will close. Answer soon.

Love,
Odis

Friday night
April 30, 1943

Dear Folks,

How are you by now? I am doing ok., except that I haven't had time to do anything. Don't be surprised if you don't hear from me very often. I am kept so busy that I don't have time to write. We got back from supper last night at 8:00 and then we had to G.I. (scrub) the barracks and we have to be in bed by ten. I guess we will get to go to town tomorrow night. I have just about enough money for bus fare there and back.

I have been up four times and I really like the airplane and my instructor never gets mad and cusses you out, although it's not too late for him to begin. We have lots to remember to do and we are going to start getting stars for our mistakes. Each star costs us 15 cents each.

If I get along ok, I hope you can come out and see me in about a month or two.

Well, I will have to close and get my footlocker in shape for Saturday morning inspection. Answer soon.

Love,
Odis

P.S. I received the $15.00 before I left Cuero.

Odis' younger brother Jack's patriotism helped him make up his mind to join the army. On May 5, 1943, he was sent to Mineral Wells, Texas to be inducted into the army. He was not as athletic as Odis and his health was not good, but he had a strong desire to serve his country.

On May 8th, he was sent to Camp Wallace, Texas, for basic training. He was able to claim he was responsible for 50% of the support of the family and they received a special allowance from the army. He also sent money home along with war bonds and instructed his dad to cash them in if needed.

By corresponding, Odis and Jack encouraged each other. Odis took his role as "big brother" seriously. He knew what Jack's new life was like, and did what he could to help him through the tough times.

Wednesday
May 12, 1943

Dear Folks,

How are you by now? I am doing ok. I am still kept jumping all the time. I flew three hours this morning and we have a lecture each day and we also have to pull chocks an hour a day so after we spend a half-day on the flight line we are tired and then drill and three hours of classes and P.T. each day keeps us going and I have to go to night classes because I have a low average in navigation. The ground school here is really rough. Of course, most of the boys have college educations and it isn't quite so rough on them.

I got a letter from Jack and he is at Camp Wallace. I don't know anything about coast artillery, but I wouldn't like it. Of course, the army is what you make it where ever you are.

We had a big rain here the other day, but it is fair and pretty now.

Well, I don't have anything to write about so I will close. Answer soon.

Love,
Odis

P.S. I had some pictures made but they don't have an airplane in them. I will get them in about a week.

Monday night
May 13, 1943

Dear Folks,

How are you by now? I received your letter today and also one from Jack. I try to write Jack as often as I can, because I know it helps a fellow if he gets a little mail all along. I sent him three or four dollars in the letters I wrote him. I didn't know how much money he had, but I knew he didn't have too much.

Well, I guess I will go on a little short dual cross country tomorrow. We will start the long solo cross countries about the last of this week. We are shooting stages these days. I guess I will be ready for my power approach tomorrow.

Are you still planning on coming out to see me? I don't know where I will be sent from here. It will most likely to Lubbock, Texas.

Well, I don't have any news so I will close. Answer soon.

Love,
Odis

Thursday
May 27, 1943

Dear Folks,

How are you by now? I am doing ok, but we have really been busy for the last week. We had out cross country to Jacksonville and Palestine yesterday and night flying last night. I got almost five hours in the air yesterday and last night. I was first to go up last night and I got to bed by eleven thirty. You can see lights all over the country for miles and it really looks pretty. I think we are going to Sight 44 in Mineral Wells tomorrow morning. Every cross country we have somebody to get lost and land somewhere way off course and there has been about a dozen that got off course and it takes an extra couple hours to get back.

I got my first instrument ride today. It's quite a bit different from link trainer.

Well, if we get our flying time in we will get a little time off about the 25th of next month. I would like to come home if I could, but if I can't that would be a good time for you to come out to see me. You probably wouldn't be allowed on the field to watch us fly anyway.

I get a letter from jack pretty often. I guess he will make it ok. He will probably be shipped across in 4 or 5 months. I got three more months training before I get my wings and they won't keep me around much longer. I'm sweating out a P-38 now. That's the only pursuit I will have a chance to fly. All AV/S get twin engine ships.

Well, I will have to close. Answer soon.

Love,
Odis

The Link Trainer was a flight simulator used to teach pilots how to fly on instruments during bad weather or at night. The enclosed trainer had a complete set of instruments and controls similar to a real cockpit. The controls could pitch, roll, dive and climb as the student operated it. The aerospace program and airlines today use flight simulators developed from the concept of the original Link Trainer.

On May 27, Odis was appointed a sergeant in the aviation cadet group. This gave him the title of Section Leader of the class. He was in charge of all under his command and was responsible for class discipline. The Section Leader was the contact between the class and the school on all orders and directions from the school.

ARMY AIR FORCES BASIC FLYING SCHOOL

Upon the recommendation of his Tactical Officer I do hereby appoint

AVIATION CADET PRIMROSE, CLYDE O. JR., a SERGEANT in the Aviation Cadet Group to rank as such from the TWENTY-SEVENTH day of MAY, 1943. He is therefore carefully and diligently to discharge his duties as SECTION LEADER, and all cadets coming under his command are strictly charged and required to be obedient to his orders as such. And he is to observe and follow such orders and directions as he shall receive from his military superiors, according to the rules and discipline of War.

Given under my hand at Waco Army Flying School, Waco, Texas, this TWENTY-SEVENTH day of MAY in the year of Our Lord one thousand nine hundred and FORTY-THREE

C D Querry

C.D. QUERRY, Major AIR CORPS,
Commandant of Aviation Cadets.

Appointment as section leader.

Friday
June 4, 1943

Dear Folks,

How are you by now? I am ok. I received all of your letters and was glad to get them. I have been so busy I haven't had time to answer them.

We had to fly last night and didn't get to bed until 2:00 and had to get up at 7:00 this morning and I am really tired tonight. We fly tomorrow morning and tomorrow night and also Sunday evening. We are way behind with our time. I lack 4 hours night flying, 3 hours formation and 12 hours dual instruments. We only have 17 more flying days before we leave here. One boy washed out today and he had 40 hours (slow progress). You don't make many mistakes around here and get by with it.

I am doing ok in ground school now. I finally wound up with an 80 average in navigation and I have an 85 average after the mid-term test in meteorology. I don't have to attend night classes anymore.

Well, I will close until next time. Answer soon.

Love,
Odis

Tuesday
June 8, 1943

Dear Folks,

How are you by now? I am doing ok. We flew last night and we made flood light landings and then landing lights. We are going on night cross country tomorrow night. I got into a little trouble the other day. I forgot to check my brakes before I landed and I landed with them locked. I was lucky I got them unlocked in time or I would have nosed over. I was landing on the concrete runway and it was a thousand wonders it didn't turn bottom side up. It's just one time out of a thousand that the brakes will get locked. I was doing acrobatics and they locked some how.

Well, we have 14 more days here and we have lots of time yet to get in. I lack two more check rides yet. Well, I guess I will close as I don't have any news and I have got to write Jack. I haven't written him in quite awhile. We fly every other night and the nights we don't fly I don't feel like writing. Answer soon.

Love,
Odis

Sunday
June 13, 1943

Dear Folks,

How are you by now? I am doing ok. I thought I would try to write you a few lines this morning. We are not flying today, but we are flying tonight. We lack two more night cross countries and one more night of blitz landings. We are through with out day cross countries and I am through with my acrobatics. I had my 40 hour check the other day and passed it. I will get an instrument check next week.

We will leave here for Lubbock about the 22nd. That will be twin engine advanced.

Well, I will have to close. Answer soon.

Love,
Odis

Wednesday
June 16, 1943

Dear Folks

How are you by now? I am doing ok. I received your letter today and was glad to hear from you.

Well, I would like to know if you could pick me up at Nacogdoches about mid-night next Monday night if I can get a pass. I have a ride to Nacogdoches if I can get a pass. I don't expect I can get over a two day if I get one at all. If I hear from you, I will call Walter Walker Monday evening to let you know I am coming. Answer as soon as possible and I will let you know by letter as soon as I find out whether I can get off or not.

Well, I will have to close as I have to get up early in the morning. Answer soon.

Love,
Odis

P. S. I am sending a small picture of me, my instructor and two other students at Primary.

Thursday
June 17, 1943

Dear Folks,

How are you by now? I am ok. I found out today that we are going to have to fly up to the day we leave here. I won't get a pass.

I had my last check ride today and we are finishing our night flying tonight. We are going to shoot blackout landings. Well, I don't have time to write a letters so I will close until next time. Answer soon.

Love,
Odis

Tuesday
June 22, 1943

Dear Folks,

How are you by now? I received your letters today and was glad to get them. I am glad you are getting along ok.
I am all through with my ground school here and I have all my required time in. I imagine I will fly about an hour tomorrow and that will be all. We shot hurdle stages today and there wasn't any wind and it was almost impossible to get it down before you got to the line which was 200 ft. past the 7 ft string we had for a hurdle. I pulled one up over the string and it stalled out and dropped about 10 ft. straight down. I wouldn't have been surprised if the landing gear had come off. I got one good one in out of 6 and only had that one bad landing.

They broke the string 6 or 8 times and one boy flew right through it and carried it off.

The orders came out today and I am going to Lubbock for sure. We will have to take a physical right after we arrive there. I hope I pass it.

We got our class books yesterday and I will try to send it to you as soon as I can get a chance to get to the post office. You won't get much good out of it. I have had the boys in my flight to sign in their nicknames, etc.

Well, I have got to close until next time.

Love,
Odis

Class picture.

CHAPTER 7

Advanced Flight Training

Odis started his final flight training at Lubbock Army Air Field in Lubbock, Texas, with Class 43H on June 28, 1943. Lubbock is located in the high plains panhandle area of Texas. It is a medium size city in the middle of very flat terrain with no trees. Most of the year it is very windy and cool at night. The daytime temperature can be over 100 degrees in middle-to-late summer.

Advanced flight training was a continuation of the same training, but in much greater complexity. As in all phases of cadet training, it consisted of ground school, physical training, inspections, etc. Flying became more difficult with detailed navigation for long distances, additional instrument flying, radio procedures with landing fields, and intensive night flying. The major difference in training was the transition to a twin engine airplane that had retractable landing gears and electrically operated flaps. Twin engine planes require the additional skill of synchronizing the speed of the two engines.

Cadets started in the slower Cessna AT-17 "Bobcat" trainer. The plane was made of wood and tubular steel with a fabric covering. This construction gave it the nickname of "Bamboo Bomber" with a second name of "Double Breasted Cub." The plane weighed 5700 pounds, had two 245HP Jacobs engines and had a maximum speed of 175 MPH. The landing speeds were relatively slow, similar to the planes in primary and basic training.

The next plane the cadets used in training was the Curtiss AT-9 "Fledging" nicknamed "Jeep", with all metal construction. The AT-9 weighed 6,062 pounds, was powered by two Lycoming 295 HP engines, with a maximum speed of 197 MPH. The AT-9 was a faster and more difficult twin engine trainer than the AT-17. The handling of this faster plane made it ideal training for pilots who would go on to fly high performance aircraft.

Class 43-H graduated on August 30, 1943, received their wings, and were commissioned as 2nd Lieutenants or Flight Officers (Warrant Officers). Warrant Officers were cadets who came up from the enlisted ranks. In early 1944, Flight Officers were converted to 2nd Lieutenants, in order to correct the imbalance between the two ratings. Some cadets came into the program as existing 2nd Lieutenants by transferring from army units.

The majority of new officers were sent to transition training as four engine bomber crews, and then sent to a combat unit. Some became instructors, while others transitioned to twin engine fighters or to twin engine bombers.

Sunday
June 22, 1943

Dear folks,

How are you by now? I arrived here all tired and worn out. We spent 24 hours on the train. As far as I can see so far I will like this place fine. Of course they say you are kept plenty busy for the first four weeks.

We are going to fly twin engine AT-17s. There is quite a change in the procedure here. You have two engines to contend with and retractable landing gear, electric flaps and the traffic patterns and radio procedure are quite a bit different.

Well, I have already put in my order for a graduation ring $17.00. I decided that I might as well get one. You don't graduate but once.

Well, I will write the next time I get time and let you know how I like this place. Answer soon.

Love,
Odis

Thursday
July 1, 1943

Dear Folks,

I received your letters today and was happy to hear from you. I am doing ok so far. I passed my physical exam and I have had a one hour ride. It lands and stalls a lot slower than the BT did. The procedures are kind of hard to catch on to. We never go up solo in this ship. When you get checked out, you and another student go up together.

Well, it has been trying to rain every since we have been up here and it has been cool. We wore sweaters to the flight line the other morning and we sleep under a blanket every night. We are 3300 ft above sea level up here and at Waco we were only 460 ft above sea level. The country around here is as flat as a table top. This is a pretty nice looking post and we are really fed good. We have to pay them whatever it cost them to feed us. They say it usually runs from 90 cents to a dollar a day and we draw the regular field rations which is about 61 cents a day. We have all the milk we want every meal and tomato juice and orange juice for breakfast. We have never been fed as good before. We also have an orchestra to play for us twice a week in the mess hall.

We just started our main schedule today and we are on the flight line from 7:30am to 1:00 and then we have 3 hours of ground school, one hour P.T. and then link training at night. Alternating each day, we fly in the evening one day and morning the next.

Well, I will close. Answer soon.

Love,
Odis

Saturday
July 3, 1943

Dear Folks,

How are you by now? I received your letters today and was glad to get them.

We have a few boys over 200 cadets in 43-H. I don't know who is the closest to Hemphill but I know one from Glade Water, Texas. There aren't ever any officers moved with the cadets. Officers are stationed permanently at each field. At preflight they split the groups up and sent them to different primary schools all over the Gulf Coast Training area and we were all sent to Waco from Cuero. From Waco, they were split and sent to Blockland at Waco, Foster Field (Single Engine) and here. All of the AV/S are still together what's left of us. When we leave here we will really be split up.

Well, I have 4 hours in and was ready to go up on a solo or buddy ride and the clouds moved in. The AT-17 only cruises at 140mph, or less and lands at about 40 miles an hour. We call it a double breasted cub. It will float all day. It's made of plywood and fabric. The AT-9 is an all metal ship and is the fastest landing ship the army has except the B-26, but we don't get much time in the AT-9.

Well, I will close. Answer soon.

Love,
Odis

Friday night
July 16, 1943

Dear Folks,

How are you by now? I am doing ok. I will try to answer the last letters I received from you. Nothing new has happened around here except that we are restricted on account of paralysis.

I got a letter from Lawrence and he is working in Beaumont. I guess he must be doing ok.

Do you know what kind of a ship Leon was flying when was at home? The AT-6 is usually what they pick.

Have you heard from Booley lately? I imagine he is still in pretty safe territory. I'll probably be over there by the first of the year, but not any sooner I hope.

Well, I don't have anything to write, so I will close.

Love,
Odis

Tuesday
July 20, 1943

Dear Folks,

How are you by now? I am ok. I received your letter today and was glad to hear from you.

It has been raining pretty often since I have been up here, but it hasn't kept us from flying much lately. I think we are just about up to schedule with our flying time now. We started our cross countries today. We went to Big Springs and Abilene and back and tomorrow we will go to Tucumcari, New Mexico and Amarillo and back on an instrument cross country. I think we will fly the beam all the way.

I heard from Jack nearly every week, but I don't have time to write him very often. You said that he didn't weigh but 130. He must not have gained much since he has been in the army. I am still skinny as ever, but I manage to weigh about 160 or 165 all the time.

I don't know where I will be sent from here. I also don't know what I will be flying. It could be anything from P-38's to B-24's. I don't want to have to fly the B-24's, but I had rather fly them than the B-26's. I am still hoping that there is a chance that some of us will get P-38's. I may sign up for instructor, but I know I wouldn't like that.

I don't have any news, so I will close. Answer soon.

Love,
Odis

Friday night
July 23, 1943

Dear Folks,

How are you by now? I am ok. I will try to write you a few lines. It has really been hot up here. It's the first real hot weather we have had up here. It hasn't rained in the last few days.

The restriction was lifted yesterday and I went to town to a show last night.

We have been taking XC all week and we are going to Portales, New Mexico Canyon and back tomorrow on a low altitude XC. I have 41 hours pilot time now and we only have to have 70 in all. We still lack all of our night flying and that is 20 hours. We get some pretty long night XC's. About the easiest way to get home at night when you get lost is to fly the beam.

We are almost through with the main part of our ground school, but we will have lectures the last four weeks we are here on this and that.

I have no news so will close. Answer soon.

Love,
Odis

Monday
August 2, 1943

Dear Folks,

How are you by now? I have finally found time to write you a few lines. We had to fly 4 nights last week and last night. The first night we got checked out and the next night we flew local and shot a few landings and we have been on three cross countries the other nights. We are 17 days ahead of schedule now. I have 56-1/2 hours. I finished my day transition this evening. I think that the rest of our day time will be in AT-9's, the fastest landing ship the army has except the B-26.

Our upper class graduated last week and 5 out of the class got instructors, 16 got B-26's and the rest got B-17's and B-24's. The ones that passed the pressure chamber test got to go to transition schools and the rest went straight to tactical outfits and will be co-pilots. That was the sickest bunch of boys that I ever saw when they got their orders and found out that they had to fly heavy bombers. Lots of them had put in for twin engine fighters, light bombardment or dive bombers and they were disappointed.

I was all pepped up because I got recommended for twin engine fighter, but now I am expecting the worse. There were 26 out of my squadron that was recommended for fighters and I am still hoping that we will get them.

We got paid Saturday and I had $14.95 left after all the deductions. I had to cancel my war bonds and you won't get one for August, but you will for July. As officers, we have to change all our records and start over again.

Yes, we get our wings here, but a six weeks transition school after we leave here if we don't get sent out as co-pilots.

I got the Reporter.

Talking about fun, this course is not as dry as I make it seem in my letters. I don't know about the Irish, but if you make a "crack" there is always someone of the bunch that comes back with a better one. Some one always gets mixed up and says the wrong thing over the radio during the day and he gets razzed about that. Everybody always has to tell about the jam he got into during the day. Last night most all of us got mixed up. We had to land at Abilene on a cross country and we would ask for "landing instructions and the tower told us to land on the Southeast runway and there were at least 6 that looked like they were or could be S.E. and I finally got lined up on one with my compass reading S.E. and then when we got on the ground, we did not know where we were nor which way to turn to get back to the other end of the runway. There were ships all over the field. Finally, when we got back to the take off place we switched seats and when my buddy took off we didn't go ten yards before we were off the runway in the grass headed in some direction I don't know, but we pulled it off the ground just in time to miss a bunch of lights. There were just enough runway lights to get you confused. The control officer was pulling his hair out. Everybody wanted on the radio at the same time. We had a ship coming in every two minutes and they couldn't give each ship many instructions. I know you can't understand this, but I know everything was in a mess.

I will close and go to bed and try to get a little sleep. Answer soon.

Love,

Odis

P.S. We had our pictures made tonight for our class books. I had them send my ring home if they aren't finished by the time I graduate and I will try to have enough out of my clothing allowance to pay for it. I have about half my clothes bought. I still lack quite a few small items yet. I'm not buying any tailor made clothes now, but later on I may. My coat and two pair pants only cost $42.00. Sun tan suit (shirt and pants) cost almost $30.00.

Friday
August 6, 1943

Dear Folks,

How are you by now? I am ok. and don't have time to write much. I will write you later about our big cross country we are taking tomorrow and tomorrow night.

I hope you can come out when I graduate. There's not much to the graduation exercise, but you can go around over the post and see the air planes. I think maybe my girl from Ft. Worth is coming up here, but I don't care about everybody around Hemphill knowing about it.

I may be sent to Fort Worth from here. If I am I will have to fly B-24's.

I got a card from Lawrence saying he had a big girl.

I got one Reporter, but I haven't got one for this week. Well, I will close. Answer soon.

Love,
Odis

Friday Morning
August 13, 1943

Dear Folks,

How are you by now? I am doing ok. I received the ten dollars and was really glad to get it. It looks like every time I turn around I see something else I have to buy. I'll have a little left out my clothing allotment, but we don't get that until after we graduate.

About all the flying we are doing now is night flying. We went to Albuquerque, N.M., El Paso and back last Saturday. While we were at El Paso, we went across the river into Juarez, Mexico and we flew back home Saturday night.

We are going to graduate August the 30th and I will be a flight officer. I will rank just below a 2nd Lt. and my pay will be just a little more than a 2nd Lt. I don't know just how much I will make, but it will be about $280 flying pay, quarters and rations included.

I don't have any news, so I will close until next time. Answer soon.

Love,
Odis

Monday night
August 16, 1943

Dear Folks,

How are you by now? I am doing fine. We are almost through flying. We are still flying every other night and once or twice in the day time each week. They are giving us all a check ride. I guess I will get mine Wednesday evening.

Well, the latest news is that I will go to Fort Worth and fly B-24's. That is a transition school and it will last six weeks and then we are supposed to get a furlough.

Well, we graduate the 30th and we have a graduation dance the Saturday night before. There won't be much dance to it. Everybody will be too drunk to dance. Every class up to now pulls a three day drunk for graduation and I guess it will be the same this time. My girl from Ft. Worth is coming up and stay for the dance and graduation, but I wish she wasn't.

If you will send me Mammie and Thel's address, I will send them an invitation and also Grandpa Primrose's address.

We are having some of the hottest weather out here I have ever been in. It was 112 degrees one day this week and most of the crops are burning up. It hasn't rained in over a month.

I got a letter from Westley the other day and one from Jack today, but there's so little to write about until I just hate to try to write anymore.

Well, I will close until next time.

Love,
Odis

Tuesday night
August 17, 1943

Dear Folks,

How are you by now? I am doing ok, except that I had a tooth pulled and it hurts a little. I didn't get to fly tonight on account of it. It blew up a norther and a little rain last night and it has been pretty cool all day today.

I'm glad you got to go to the show. That's what I do the nights I don't fly and when I should be writing letters.

I have not received a Reporter in a couple of weeks; in fact I only got one. I don't know whether they were sent and they got lost in the mail.

The war news looks pretty good these days. We may finish this thing up in two or three years. There are five boys in my barracks that came from New Guinea and what they say fighting the Japs is not the way most people have it figured. One of the boys was telling me that the Japs would get out a little ways from a dugout or trench and call for "Cpl. White" or make some racket and try to get you to stick your head up and then shoot you. He says he had sat out lots of nights and watched flares go up, maybe 4 or maybe 3 forming a square or triangle showing the Jap bombers where to bomb and he said they always bombed the most vital places. He said lots of times they would wake up and hear Jap bombers and just roll over and go back to sleep. He said they use to set around at night and listen to the planes and identify them by the sound. He said they got to where they knew what was coming as soon as they could hear them. These boys were across almost a year and they haven't had a furlough since they got back and aren't going to get any more furloughs than the rest of us get. You are supposed to get a 30 day furlough after you get back from foreign duty, but your back furlough time is canceled when you become an officer.

Well, I will close until next time. Answer soon.

Love,
Odis

Lubbock
August 31, 1943

Dear Folks,

I have finally found time to write you a few lines. I never signed so many papers and forms in my life as I have the last three days. We had to start out new again and all of our papers had to be changed.

We got the nastiest deal that has ever been handed out to a bunch of men at this school. I am going to the Second Air force at Clovis New Mexico as a co-pilot on a consolidated liberator B-24. We don't know a thing, but rumor, but I think a little later on if you are good enough you make first pilot. All the second air force goes to Australia, so I know where I will go when I go across. I will have at least 3 months before I go across (I hope) and we are supposed to get furloughs before we leave.

Well, I will have to close. I will write you just as soon as I get to Clovis. Answer soon.

Love,
Odis

When an enlisted man is promoted to the Officer Corps, he is discharged from the army on paper and re-enlisted immediately as an officer. This procedure created a large amount of paperwork.

The Lubbock Army Air Field

of

Lubbock, Texas

announces the graduation of

Class 43-H

Monday morning, August thirtieth

nineteen hundred and forty-three

at ten o'clock

Graduation invitation.

Flight Officer Primrose after receiving his wings.

CHAPTER 8

Clovis, New Mexico

Flight officer, Odis Primrose arrived at the 2nd Air Force, 302nd Bomb Group Army Air Force Base Clovis, New Mexico, where he was placed in a B-24 bomber crew. Clovis is located in a very hot and arid area next to the Texas border northeast of Lubbock. The 302nd bomb group was a collection and assembly point for pilots and crews prior to being sent to units or transition training as complete crews. Bomb groups were being activated and trained as units prior to going overseas to combat. Crews not needed for unit fills were sent to replacement training units (RTU) for crew transition training.

The Clovis Army Airfield was a hastily constructed facility with many buildings built with wood frames and covered with tar paper. Some buildings were more permanent in nature, but facilities were lacking. Time was spent on paperwork, lectures, link training, bomb training, and organizing crews.

Odis was assigned to crew #302-9-71 with First Lieutenant John McLaughlin as pilot. The remainder of his crew were 2nd Lieutenant Carl G. Walker as bombardier and Sergeants Anthony Kosak, Lowell Root, Roy Maxwell, Melvin Fover, and James Reese. The navigator and one additional enlisted man did not join the crew until final group assignment. At this stage of training, Odis had never seen a B-24 or flown in a four engine plane.

On August 15, 1943, special orders #258 transferred his crew to the 450th Heavy Bomb group in Alamogordo, New Mexico. The 450th BG was activated as a new group on paper at Gowan Field at Boise, Idaho, on May 1, 1943 without personnel or equipment. On May 31, 1943, the new designated group was assigned to Clovis Army Air Base, and on June 1, Captain William Snaith was appointed temporary commander of the group until Colonel Mills arrived on June 12. (Much more about Capt. Snaith later.) Key staff and other personnel started arriving during this short period.

On June 22, the key staff moved to Orlando, Florida, in four B-24D aircraft to attend the Applied Tactics School for advanced training. This training would give them the skills to become an operational combat unit. The remainder of the group moved from Clovis to the Air Force Base in Alamogordo, New Mexico, on July 5 to set up housekeeping and prepare for the arrival of the new personnel.

Alamogordo is located in the desert on the southeast section of White Sands and in the Tularosa Basin between two mountain ranges. This base was 85 miles north of El Paso, Texas, and 60 miles south of the site where the first atomic bomb was exploded. The Alamogordo Army Air Base is now Holloman Air Force Base. This base was used in the early days of research for space flight. Rocket sleds were used to test acceleration on the body that would occur in lift off into space. Numerous high altitude balloons were sent aloft from this site.

Clovis Army Air Base
Clovis, New Mexico.
Thursday
September 2, 1943

Dear Folks,

How are you by now? I am doing ok. I am just about to get settled, but I haven't gotten all of my luggage yet. We arrived here Tuesday evening and this place don't look so good. We have tar paper barracks and they burn soft coal here and smut flies every where. We stay two men to a room in BOQ (Bachelor Officer's Quarters). Laundry service is bad. It takes 10 days to get laundry back and a week to get cleaning back. Most of us fellows only have 3 or 4 suits of kakis and I imagine it will be kindly rough to keep clean clothes. We had to pay $34.50 cash just as soon as we got here for officer's mess tickets for one month and the food isn't as good as we had at Lubbock. We have a nice officer's club here on the post and they are having a dance there tonight, but I can't dance yet.

There is a big drive on in heavy bombardment and the most of us fellows will make first pilot before we go across (3 to 6 months) and we are promised a leave before we go across. They are taking men out of single engine schools and making them co-pilots in B-24's. It's a known fact that they have quit building B-17's & I am glad that I am flying

B-24's. I would like to get into the new B-29 school because it is a new and coming thing and I would like to get in on the ground floor. I have been through A. M. school and that will help. I am still pretty young yet. There's not too many guys that get their wings before they are 21. Jack sent me three dollars and I really appreciated it because I knew he didn't have much money. Dixie sent me seven dollars.

Well, I guess I will have to close. I have to get up and get shaved and eat breakfast and be down at the processing center by 7:30 tomorrow morning. Answer soon.

Love
Odis

P.S. If you have time you might drop in and let the Reporter know my new address. I might not be here but 3 to 8 weeks. We have 3 places to go before we are ready to go across.

Sunday night
September 5, 1943

Dear Folks,

How are you by now? I am doing ok. I received the ten dollars yesterday and was very glad to get it. I wasn't broke, but I expect it will come in handy before the month is up.

Boy, I mean this place is dry up here. It came up a small shower yesterday evening and that is the only cloud I have seen since I have been here.

We are in processing center now, but we get out tomorrow night. We have been going to lectures, having drill and P.T., but we never go to P.T. or drill. I don't know when we will start flying.

Have you heard from Westley lately? I got a letter from him at Lubbock, but I have not answered it yet.

Do you know where Capt. Leon is now? I wouldn't doubt but what he is across by now. I have quite a ways to go before I am a Captain. I am a flight officer now and next comes Second Lt. I am making one dollar a month now more than a 2nd Lt., but you have to be a second before first, usually.

Well, I can't think of a thing to write, so I will close. Answer soon.

Love,
Odis

Monday
September 6, 1943

Dear Folks,

I received your letter this morning I hope Dot gets well ok.

My girl didn't come out to the graduation from Ft. Worth. Her girl friend backed out and wouldn't come out with her and she couldn't stay for nothing but the dance so I sent her a telegram and told her not to come. I took one of the Lubbock girls to the dance and we had a big time.

I hope Jack gets his furlough. I don't know when I will get one. Clovis is only a hundred miles northwest of Lubbock. Every time I move I get further away from home. The next time I move I will be quite a ways from home. I don't think I will be here very long. We have 4 phases before we go across. The first is the pilots phase, second is bombing and the last is navigation.

Boy, it blew up a sandstorm from the north last night and it was pretty cool this morning. I had to buy me a jacket this morning.

Well, I have no news so I will close until next time. Answer soon.

Love,
Odis

Wednesday
September 8, 1947

Dear Folks,

How are you by now? I am ok. I received a letter from you yesterday and one today. I don't think you got one of my letters I wrote you from indications in your letter. I got the $10.00 the day after I got here.

Well, I have been here a week and I haven't had a ride and I'm not scheduled tomorrow. They are awfully crowded and are shipping a few men out. If I stay here as much as a month more I will probably leave as first pilot, but if I am shipped in the next day or so, I will be a co-pilot. I would still have a chance to becoming a first pilot.

We are sleeping under two blankets every night up here, but it is pretty warm in the evenings. This country is flat and there aren't any mountains around here close. There are some up close to Albuquerque.

Well, I don't have any news so I will have to close for this time. Answer soon.

Love,
Odis

Saturday
September 11, 1943

Dear Folks,

How are you by now? I am doing ok. All I am doing these days is taking link training and bomb training. I just get off my bed enough so that the Negro boy can make it up every morning. I have been up at the officer's club playing cards all evening, but I have got bomb training from 9:00 to 10:00 tonight.

I hated to hear about Pete's daddy. If you see Pete, tell him that I'll write him if I ever stay in one place long enough to get an answer from him.

I have got two letters from Jack since I have been here and he seems to be getting along ok. I know I would if I was in Chicago. I know he will make out ok until his money runs out.

I have been assigned to a crew of about 10 men and I haven't seen any of them yet. I still haven't been up in a B-24. My First pilot is a 1st Lt. They are shipping 8 crews out the 15th and my crew is a star crew and will be shipped if anyone is shipped. I guess you have figured out by now that I am to be the co-pilot in this crew. We have been trying to slip around and find out where we are going, but don't know yet. Don't be surprised if it is a long way off.

I received the clipping and I knew Reynolds and Lahaye. I don't know when we had those pictures made, but I don't think much of them.

If the Reporter is ever sent here and I am gone, they won't forward it and I'll never get it.

Well, I will close this and go down to bomb training. Answer real soon.

Love,
Odis

CHAPTER 9

The B-24 Bomber

Special assignment orders had been issued to transfer Odis and his crew to the Alamogordo Army Air Base in New Mexico with September 27, 1943 as their report date. This meant they would be flying the B-24 bombers.

Flight Officer Odis Primrose still had never seen a B-24 and had never even been in a four engine plane. The pilot, John McLaughlin had just completed a twenty-one day transition school qualifying him to be a four engine pilot, but he did his training in the B-17. Prior to this, Lt. McLaughlin had graduated from twin engine training and received his wings in early spring. By August 1943, he also had never been in a B-24. The new assignment in this unfamiliar plane proved to be a very fast and intensive learning experience for all the crew.

The B-24 Liberator, designed by Consolidated, was produced in greater quantities and flew in more theaters of the war than any other four engine bomber during WWII. A total production of 19,256 planes was accomplished by Consolidated-Vultee of San Diego and Fort Worth, Ford Motor Co. at Willow Run, Douglas Aircraft in Tulsa, North American Aircraft in Dallas, and Convair in Fort Worth. Douglas in Tulsa and Consolidated in Fort Worth primarily built subassemblies for other plants, but also built complete planes.

The B-24 had a wingspan of 110', was 63'9" long, and was approximately 18' tall. Its gross weight was 65,000 lbs. loaded, and had a top speed of 306 MPH, a ceiling of 31,500ft, a range of 3,000 miles loaded, and was powered by four Pratt and Whitney Model R-1830 engines rated at 1200HP each. The front, top, rear, and belly turrets of each were armed with dual .50 caliber machine guns. The two waist positions had one .50 caliber machine gun each. The initial cost was $336,000 or the equivalent of $3,900,000 in today's dollars. (2008)

The B-24 was a self contained air plane that did not require outside auxiliary power to start the engines. A gasoline power unit inside the plane was used in conjunction with the batteries to start the engine. This unit was known as a "putt-putt" due to the way it sounded. It would be cut off after the engines started. In order to avoid damage to the engine, the propellers on each engine had to be pulled full circle to clean any accumulated oil or fuel from the combustion chambers prior to starting.

The secret to the success of the B-24 was the patented design of the wing by David Davis. The long, slim, low drag wing made the plane highly maneuverable. The location of the wing high on the fuselage gave more room in the inside for transport uses. The wings could actually wave up and down in bad weather. Two life rafts were located in compartments just above the wing in case the plane had to be ditched at sea. An escape hatch was also located behind the cockpit to be used in ditching.

The B-24 was somewhat of a stepchild during WWII, as the B-17 received all the attention and publicity. The B-17 was used primarily from England in the strategic air campaign against the Germans in Europe. B-24s were also flown out of England, but in much smaller numbers than the B-17. The majority of the war correspondents worked out of England and continuously reported back on the wonderful "Fortress Bomber". The B-24 was faster, had heavier bomb load, was more maneuverable, and had a much longer range than the B-17. The only advantage of the B-17 was an extra 3,000' operational ceiling which allowed better protection from enemy anti-aircraft fire.

The B-24, which had an unusual twin tail, was built as a bomber, and also configured as a military passenger plane, cargo plane, and fuel tanker. The single tail model was built as a bomber for the navy. The wide body gave it nick names such as "Flying Box Car" or "Pregnant Cow". This adaptability allowed the Liberator to be successful serving in a wide variety of roles, such as bomber, maritime reconnaissance, attacking "U" boats in the Atlantic and Gulf waters, transport, service, and photographic reconnaissance. The long range capability was suited for missions from North Africa to the Ploesti oil fields, and long over-water missions in the Pacific theater. The B-24 could also be fitted with long range fuel tanks in the bomb bay for additional extension of range.

LB-30 Liberator (Early Model B-24) Confederate Air Force.

Interior of B-24 cockpit.

B-24D in the U.S. Air Force Museum.

The normal bomb load was 5,000 lbs, but for a short mission with a smaller fuel load, 6,000 lbs would be carried. The normal bombs were general purpose, with the early ones loaded with TNT, and later, with the sensitive explosive RDX. TNT needed an armed fuse to set it off, whereas RDX would explode from a hard blow. General purpose bombs were 100 lbs, 500 lbs, 1,000 lbs and 2,000 lbs. The fuse had a small propeller that would spin in the air when released, arming the bomb at a safe distance from the plane. The regular fuse would detonate on contact, but special delay fuses were also used. A delay would be used to cause the bomb to penetrate a structure before going off. Also, long delays would go off after the bombing raid, catching repair crews going to work.

Special bombs were used for other devastating purposes. General purpose bombs used by the first planes would be followed by fire bombs to set the destroyed material on fire. Fire bombs were also used on cities. Fragmentation bombs, similar to bundles of hand grenades, were used against personnel and parked air planes.

The fully armed and combat ready plane carried a crew of ten men. The crew was made up of pilot, co-pilot, bombardier, and navigator, who were commissioned officers. The enlisted crew consisted of an engineer who also operated the top turret, a radio operator who also operated as a waist gunner, an assistant engineer who also operated as a waist gunner, one gunner who operated the nose turret, one gunner who operated the tail turret, and a remaining gunner who operated the ball turret.

The pilot and co-pilot operated from the flight deck, with the pilot in the left seat. The flight deck was the only compartment that had an in-flight heater. During take offs, landings, and in flight, the flight engineer would be behind the pilot assisting with fuel transfer and other duties, when not operating the top gun turret. The radio operator was also located behind the co-pilot, when not working as waist gunner. The navigator worked in the nose section, outfitted with an astrodome for sextant readings and side windows for outside visibility. In normal formation flying, only the lead plane navigator did the navigation for the entire group. The navigators of the other planes had to be prepared to take over if the lead plane was shot down, or if his plane had to leave formation and fly back for any reason.

The bombardier was responsible to see that the bombs were loaded correctly and fused. He normally stayed behind the flight deck to remove the safety pins from the fuse after take off. When the plane got close to the target, he would move to his position in the nose to turn on the bomb sight. Generally, the bombardier in the lead aircraft was the only one to actually sight with the bombsight. The planes following in formation would drop the bombs when they saw the first bombs drop from the lead plane. This was called "toggling" the bombs. Other bombardiers were prepared in case the lead plane was lost prior to bombing.

The primary bombsight was the Norden, and a second bombsight was the Sperry. The most common sight in the 450th was the Norden. However, some thought the Sperry was more accurate. The theory of bombing is similar to the ballistics of the artillery shell, but far more complicated. The falling bomb must be released at the correct distance from the target to account for gravity, airspeed, wind speeds, air resistance, cross winds, ballistics of the bomb type, sighting angle, and side drift of the airplane. The sights were stabilized in position by gyroscopes, and had a rudimentary computer to solve all the problems in delivery of the bomb to the target.

The B-24 had a bailout alarm that was activated in case of a fatal anti-aircraft hit, or damage from fighters. A serious hit to the airplane from either source gave only a minute or less to bailout. The plane would blow up or go into a spin. The centrifugal force of the spin would pin the crew down making it impossible for them to bail out. The crew in the nose used the nose wheel doors to bail out, the members of the flight deck and center section used the bomb bay doors, and the tail gunner or waist gunner used the photography hatch in the rear. Sometimes the waist gunners would jump through the waist gun opening or the bomb bay. In all of the escape avenues a crew member sometimes would catch in the narrow opening due to the bulkiness of his parachute which was strapped over full flying gear and a life preserver.

A detailed bail out check list and procedure was developed for the B-24, but was found to be useless. When a B-24 was hit and caught on fire, there would be only seconds before the plane exploded. The crewmen bailed out with everything on, leaving without taking time to unplug the oxygen or intercom system. One fear was that the parachute would catch fire or hang on something, pinning them in the plane.

The first models of the B-24 built in San Diego were designated LB-30s. The LB-30 Liberators went to England for the Royal Air Force in June of 1940 to assist with the war in Europe. These were the first Liberators to go into combat situations. The first Liberators the Army Air Force received in any quantity was in 1940. These were B-24D models built by Consolidated in San Diego.

The first B-24 in U.S. Service to be destroyed by enemy fire was a B-24A model at Hickam Field on December 7, 1941. In January of 1942, B-24s were used in combat for the first time, along with a group of B-17s, on a mission to the Celebes. The next major U. S. combat mission using B-24s was a raid from Egypt in June, 1942, on the Ploesti, Romania Oil Fields. This raid was called HALPRO using additional fuel tanks in the bomb bays allowing the planes to fly on to Iraq after bombing Ploesti. This was carried out by 13 B-24s with crews who had actual combat experience. The raid did little damage to the target, but gave a wake-up call to the Germans.

In September of 1942, the first B-24s started arriving in England to join the B-17 units of the 8th AF that had arrived in August. The first B-24 mission to Europe from England was in October. The 15th AF was activated November 1, 1943, to bomb areas the 8th AF could not reach. The B-24s of the 15th AF started arriving in Italy in November with missions to Europe starting that same month. The 15th AF was made up of 16 B-24 groups and six B-17 groups.

CHAPTER 10

Training As a Bomb Group

In accordance to orders #258, twenty-three crews were transferred from the Clovis Air Base to Alamogordo, New Mexico where they were assigned to the 450th Bomb Group (H). They reported September 27, 1943, to begin training as a combat group prior to being assigned to overseas duty. The group contained 60 plus planes and crews. Orders #58 by the 450th assigned crews to one of four squadrons. Crew number 302-9-3 was assigned to the 722nd squadron. The crew was listed as follows:

1st Lt. John McLaughlin, 0661518, pilot
Flight Officer Clyde O. Primrose, T-122559, co-pilot
2nd Lt. Carl G. Walker, 0749629, bombardier from Louisiana
Sgt. Anthony J. Kosak, 31211476, engineer.
Sgt. Lowell E. Root, 35157141, radio/gunner
Sgt. Roy D. Maxwell, 35589783, asst. engineer/gunner
Sgt. Melvin Fouer, 15354263, aerial gunner
Sgt. James Reese, 33497166, armorer/aerial gunner
Sgt. Albert Slinkerd, 39259671, asst. engineer/gunner

The only crew member not present was 2nd Lt. George L. Decker from New York State, who along with the other navigators, was assigned at a later date.

Each of the four squadrons of the 450th designed the name insignia for their unit. 722nd Bomb Squadron was called the "Holy Joe" Squadron. The insignia was made into a 5" diameter cloth patch which was sewn onto the leather jackets of the crew. Inside the disc was an angel clothed in white, holding a bomb in position to be dropped. A small cord hanging from the angel's belt held three playing cards, a seven and two twos, thus 722. The angel had a background of red, white and blue.

The original base was planned for two squadrons and had insufficient room or runways for four squadrons. At first, some crews were housed in tents. A rapid building program was started to build additional buildings, most of which were wooden frames covered with tar paper. The desert heat, along with the lack of cooling facilities, made life unpleasant until cool weather arrived.

The training was on an accelerated schedule to get the group combat ready and deployed to Europe as soon as possible. Training was divided into four phases, with flying and ground school mixed in each phase. The first phase was designed to increase individual job proficiency, develop team work, and to become familiar with equipment. Pilots and co-pilots were getting their first experience with the B-24. Lt. McLaughlin had to learn how to land the B-24, with its tricycle landing gear, which was totally different from the tail wheel of the B-17 he had trained on. Only the essential crew flew, while the remainder attended schools in their specialty to hone skills.

The second phase used the complete crew for bombing practice, extensive air to ground gunnery and air to air gunnery on towed targets. Some simulated bomb runs covered long distances at altitudes as high as 20,000 feet, while on oxygen. The third phase consisted of navigational skills at all altitudes, over long distances. The final phase was primarily close formation flying combined with navigation, simulated bomb runs, and flying at different altitudes. All the practice runs in phases two through four were conducted both day and night.

The group had been training with older B-24D models, but during the first part of November. new B-24H models started arriving. They were issued to the crews in preparation for movement overseas. The new planes had to be serviced and checked out prior to acceptance by the government. Odis and his crew were assigned B-24H number 42-7731. The new plane had been built in the Ford factory at Willow Run, Michigan, and then sent to a modification center in Birmingham, Alabama. After modification, the new B-24H arrived at Alamogordo on November 1, 1943. The new plane was named "Janner," probably by the pilot.

Crew of "Janner" prior to movement overseas. Back row left to right: Unidentified, unidentified, Sgt. James Reese, unidentified, unidentified, unidentified. Front row left to right: Co-pilot Flight Officer, Clyde Odis Primrose, Pilot 1st Lt. John McLaughlin, Bombardier 2nd Lt. Carl Walker, Navigator 2nd Lt. George Decker.

The completion of training for the 450th started the first phase of movement overseas. On November 19, 1943, special orders #309 were issued for the phased movement of ten crews per, day for six days, to the Army Air Base at Herington, Kansas. This was a movement by aircraft only with personal luggage.

Alamogordo Army Base
Sunday
September 28, 1943

Dear Folks,

How are you by now? I am doing ok. I am just now getting started to work around this place. We fly 6 hour missions around this place and I mean I am really tired when I get down from a flight. I had to fly form 7 to 1 o'clock last night and 1:00 to

6:39 today and I am scheduled for tomorrow evening. I have to go to ground school at 7:00 in the morning.

Have you heard from Jack lately? I haven't except some old letters. I guess he figured I wasn't going to write him, so he quit writing me. I guess he is still planning on a furlough.

Well, I am going to get all fixed up to go overseas. There's no limit as for as I know on the baggage we can carry over with us and I am going to try to carry everything I will need. I think we will go over to England, I hope, before Christmas, but you can't ever tell what they will do with us. I am in the 450th bomb group and I will move with the 450th. It will still be the 450th when we get across. I hope they put us on patrol duty for a month or two before we cross. Well, I don't have any news so I will close. Answer soon.

Love,
Odis

Thursday
October 8, 1943

Dear Folks,

How are you by now? I am doing ok. I didn't go to the hospital and have been so busy this week to think about feeling bad.

I have flown two bombing missions at 20,000 feet and it didn't seem to affect me, so I guess I will be alright. They have put a maximum on our time now. Sixty hours a month and I have already got 21 hours this week and I have a 400 mile navigation mission tomorrow morning to fly. I have put in more time this week than any other man in the squadron or group. We are short two co-pilots and I was the first to be checked out. I guess I'll like this place ok as long as they keep me busy, although I would like a day off every once in awhile. I tried to get a 24 hour pass so that I could go to El Paso and get me some clothes, but no soap this week, maybe next week.

I got a letter from Jack, but haven't had time to answer it. I should write Westley, but it seems that I never can get around to it. I'm glad Booley is doing ok. I imagine he has been in the same place long enough to get to know some people over there and that helps a lot.

Well, I guess I'll close and try to get my three hours sleep for tonight. Answer real soon.

Love,
Odis

Friday
October 15, 1943

Dear Folks,

How are you by now? I have been grounded a couple of days on account of a bad cold, but they haven't sent me to the hospital yet. I received your letter today and was glad to hear from you. I just finished a letter to Jack. I got one letter from him since I have been here.

I am glad you are going to buy the place and I wish I could send you some money to help pay for it, but it seems like its gong to take all I have for the next two months to get fixed up for overseas duty.

We never know when we will be shipped out, but I won't be here more than a month and we are going to the staging area from here where we will probably get a month's patrol duty before we go over.

I am well satisfied in the crew I'm in and I think we will make the grade if any of them do. We are supposed to get our ships soon and we won't have to worry about riding troop trains anymore.

Well, as I am short on news I will close for this time. Answer soon.

Love,
Odis

Monday
October 25, 1943

Dear Folks,

How are you all by now? I am doing ok, except that I have a cold, but I am flying. I received a letter from you today and I was very glad to hear from you. If I don't watch myself I'll be starting your letters off like I do the ones to all my girls(3). I got a letter from Jack tonight.

It's really cold up here now in the mornings. I wear my sheep skin fur lined flying jacket every morning and when I fly I put everything on. I can hardly walk with it all on. We wear the same things we wore all last winter over our regular clothes and sweater. The pilot and co-pilot have the warmest spot in the ship, but at high altitude I still sit up there and look at the temperature gauge which says 20 degrees below and shiver. At night is the only time I get cold with all my clothes on.

We are getting everything ready to leave out, but we don't know when we are leaving. We haven't got our regular ship yet. My pilot is a 1st Lt. and we led a flight of four ships on a simulated bombing mission this morning and we hit our target only about a minute late and that is extra good. Our navigator was sick the whole flight, but we made it fine and got some compliments on our formation when we came in over the field to land.

I am glad you bought the place and if you need to go ahead and cash the bonds because I don't think I will be able to send you any money for the next couple of months. I got one dollar to last me until payday, but it's not so bad, because all the other boys are broke. If they weren't I could borrow some. I got $15 loaned out and I owe $10.

How are Clara and the baby getting along? Which is it a boy or girl? I forgot.

Well, I guess I'll close and get a little shut eye. We always have to get up at 6:00 if not at 5:00. We don't fly until tomorrow afternoon, so I don't have to get up until 6:00 tomorrow morning. Write when you can.

Love,
Odis

Saturday
November 6, 1943

Dear Folks,

How are you doing by now? I am doing ok. I got a letter from you today and was glad to hear from you. I also got a letter from Jack and he said he might be sent to Fort Bliss at El Paso and if he is, we may get to see each other before I have to leave here the 20th.

We have just about caught up with our local flying and are flying simulated formation bombing missions of which you spend about five hours on oxygen. I was grounded for the flight day before yesterday and today almost all of my crew was grounded.

We took a cross country last week and we got a fuel leak on the flight deck and we landed at Colorado Springs and had dinner there. That place is right at the foot of Pikes Peak. There is snow on top of all those high mountains up there. Since then we flew to Oklahoma City via Wichita Kansas and back but nothing went wrong and we didn't get to land.

I intended to send a little money home this month, but my pilot got in a tight and I had to lend him a hundred dollars which put me a little short.

It's really cold up here in the mornings, but it warms up pretty quick after the sun comes out.

I bought me a new wrist watch and it's really a good one for the price. I only gave $30.00 for it, tax exempted, but it is anti-magnetic, water proof and will stand altitude so they told me. I haven't been up with it yet. It's a 17 jewel watch. It hasn't got much of a band on it and I figured I was buying all watch and not paying for some fancy band.

Well, I'll close for this time and try to write more often. Answer soon.

Love,
Odis

Odis was very fortunate to be able to visit his younger brother, Jack, at Ft. Bliss, El Paso, Texas. For security reasons, the 450th sealed their base one week before leaving for overseas. No one could leave. It was only a matter of days after Jack arrived at Ft. Bliss until Odis' base was sealed.

The lack of letters testifies to the intensive day and night training at Alamogordo. The crews were being prepared to go directly into combat when they arrived in Europe. The long training missions at high altitudes, and classroom lectures day and night were exhausting. The goal was to mold each crew into a tightly knit group, where each man knew his job, and could do it without assistance. In combat, a crewman must operate by instinct to meet any situation he might encounter.

CHAPTER 11

Preparation for Overseas

Special Orders #309 were issued to move the 450th to the army air base at Herington, Kansas, a staging area for overseas movement. The move would be in stages, and would start November 20, 1943. The following ten crew members and other individuals were listed for travel on ship #42-7731:

1st Lt. John McLaughlin	Sgt. Albert Slinkard
Flight Officer Clyde O. Primrose	Sgt. Melvin Fouer
2nd Lt. George L. Decker	Sgt. James L. Reese
2nd Lt Carl G. Walker	S/Sgt. Russell S. Lyon
Sgt. Anthony J. Kosak	Cpl. Juan R. Stoutt
Sgt. Lowell El Root	PFC Robert E. Glenn
Sgt. Roy D. Maxwell	Sgt. John A. Lockwood

The additional members included the ground crew chief, two ground crew members, and an additional radioman. Second Lt. George Decker, the navigator, had been added to the crew earlier and is now listed. S/Sgt Lyon, the crew chief, along with his crew, would be in charge of the maintenance of the plane on the ground.

On November 22, the remaining ground echelon was issued orders to prepare for movement by train on November 26 for Camp Patrick Henry, Virginia. Each unit was to bring all organizational equipment with them. (Tents, mess equipment, office equipment, maintenance equipment, toilet paper, etc.) Upon arrival in Virginia, the party would embark on the ships S.S. Bret Harte, U.S.S. Henry Baldwin, and the Benjamin S. Milam which would take them to the combat zone.

Odis and his crew arrived in Herington, Kansas, on the afternoon of November 23. The first order of the day was to settle in and prepare paperwork for allotments sent home, war bonds, wills, and power of attorney. Odis signed up to send a $100 bond and a $75 allotment home each month.

The crew then spent as much time as possible outfitting the plane for overseas. The plane was checked and double checked for possible problems. Some of the overseas legs such as crossing the Atlantic were very long and everything had to work perfect prior to leaving.

Equipment was the next phase of processing for movement. The crews were issued flight clothing consisting of a sheepskin coat and leg-zippered pants, fur lined helmet, steel helmet, boots, and goggles. A .45 Caliber pistol with shoulder holster was issued for personal armament. Electrically heated under suits were issued with gloves and felt shoes to wear inside of fur lined boots. Other miscellaneous gear was issued, such as oxygen masks, flak vests, and life vests. New parachutes were issued as two types, chest and seat. The pilots were issued "seat packs" that were worn all of the time. The remaining crew wore the "chest packs," which were only used during emergency. A harness was worn with it allowing the chute to be snapped on with two buckles. This system allowed freedom of movement during flight.

Herington Army Air Base
Herington, Kansas
Wednesday
November 23, 1943

Dear Folks,

How are you by now? I am doing fine. We arrived here about one o'clock today and as much as I can find out about this place, I think I am gong to like it fine and wish I could stay here as much as a week anyway, but I have some moving around to do in the next couple of weeks.

We left Alamogordo this morning in formation and ran into some bad weather and split up right away and planes are still coming in. We were the first to get here. We flew over Wichita and I saw some of those B-29's sitting on the ground.

I got to go down to see Jack before I left and he was doing ok then. They were lying around the shacks dodging KP and details. I hope he gets a furlough before long and I'm almost certain he will get one before he goes overseas.

I am sending two receipts for my allotments and I am keeping receipts.

Well, I have no news. I'll close and write you from my next stop. There's no use writing me here, just wait until you get a card with my APO number on it and then write.

Lots of Love,
Odis

Monday
November 29, 1943

Dear Folks,

How are you by now? I am dong ok now. We aren't doing anything but making two roll calls a day. We were delayed on account of some new modifications that came out. I guess we will be leaving soon.

I am sending my will and power of attorney to you and you can have them registered in the courthouse.

You will have to send Jack and all the folks my address when you get the address, because I only sent you a card.

It is pretty cold up here, but not as cold as I expected it to be. We have had frost every morning. That's something we didn't have at Alamogordo. It was too dry down there.

I think we will have a nice trip going across. I can't tell you where we are going, but we really cover some country.

Well, I don't have a thing to write about so I guess I will close. Answer soon.

Love,
Odis

Sunday night
December 5, 1943

Dear Folks,

How are you by now? Fine I hope. I am doing ok. I haven't received any letters since I have been here and I won't until I get overseas, as the mail you have sent me to my new address is on its way over now. Maybe I will get it by Christmas.

We have had quite a bit of trouble getting our ship in shape and our group has already left and some of them may be over already. We don't have much to do but make two roll calls a day and test hop our ship every now and then. We had to fly over Topeka and get a part one day and our bombardier sent for his wife and he and I hired a fellow to drive us over to Kansas City Friday night to get her and the night before that I went down to Wichita and I had a big time and last night I went to town and didn't get to bed until about 3 o'clock and had to get up at 6:30 this morning to test hop the ship. Last night was the first time I had been to bed since last Wednesday night. We have been expecting to leave every day for a week and we finally got the ship ready and our bags packed and ready to load today and the Col. is not clearing any ships tomorrow.

The wind is blowing out of the north and its raining tonight. I imagine it will really be cold tomorrow morning, but I don't think it will sleet or snow.

I hope you all have a good Christmas. I'm not expecting to have much of a Christmas this year, so I am celebrating now.

Well, there's no news so I will close. Answer soon.

Love,
Odis

The 450th group planes first left Alamogordo on November 20, 1943, and the first plane arrived in Manduria, Italy, on December 20, 1943. Due to many problems en route, such as bad weather and mechanical problems, the final planes did not arrive until the first of February, 1944. While waiting to be equipped in Herington, new modifications became available, adding additional delays. Some vital replacement parts were slow to arrive at the base, further delaying take off for overseas.

CHAPTER 12

The Trip Over

Odis and his crew left Herington, Kansas, on December 7, 1943 for Morrison Field at West Palm Beach, Florida, their port of embarkation. Crews were now assigned to the Caribbean wing of the Air Transport Command (ATC). The ATC operated bases along the route to the war zone to transport men and supplies, and to assist bomber crews. The Caribbean wing operated bases on the southern route down the Caribbean coast. At this point, the air crews had no knowledge of where they were going and were only given a heading. The sealed orders were given to the crews just before take off for each leg of the journey. The orders were marked "Secret" and could not be opened until they had been in the air for two hours.

The Caribbean wing of the ATC operated for flights using the southern route to cross over from South America to Africa, and then on to Italy or England. Some flights from Africa continued on to China. The North Atlantic wing operated for flights up the East Coast through Newfoundland to the Azores. From the Azores the planes went on to England or Africa. The North Atlantic route was notorious for severe weather, and many planes were lost due to the blinding storms and wing icing.

Odis and his crew left on the first leg of the long journey to the combat zone on December 10, 1943. The flight was approximately 1700 miles to Waller Field on the island of Trinidad. Trinidad is a small island in the West Indies, just off the coast of Venezuela. This first leg took ten and one-half hours. The second leg was approximately 1200 miles to Belem, Brazil. This flight took seven and one half hours. This leg of the journey took them over jungle and across the mouth of the Amazon River. Several B-24s went down in the Amazon jungle due to bad weather or mistakes in navigation. As late as 1995, a B-24 was found in the Brazilian jungle and the remains recovered. On the third leg they flew over 1,000 miles to Natal, Brazil. This took approximately six hours and was also over the jungle, where there was no place to land if trouble developed in the plane.

Natal was one of two jumping off places for the long over-water flight to Africa. All equipment had to be in perfect working order. Crews were involved in special meetings for pilots, navigators, and radio operators. All fuel tanks would need to be topped off to the maximum capacity while on the runway. Natal was a better base than others, with adequate facilities and food. The meals consisted mostly of fresh fruits, such as pineapples. Most crew members purchased handmade boots for $7.00, which became part of their uniform. Some crew members also purchased pet spider monkeys to take with them. Malaria tablets were issued due to the high rate of malaria in East Africa.

Wednesday
December 22, 1943

Dear Folks,

How are you by now? I am dong ok. I have been around since you last heard from me. I can't write much of anything, that's the main reason I haven't written before.

I have been in several countries since I left the states on the 10th and am somewhere in Brazil now and I guess I will be here over Christmas. I won't get any mail until I get to my final destination and it may be quite awhile before I get there. I stopped in one place for eight days and that was the biggest vacation I have had in a long time.

I hope Jack has got a furlough by now. It would be nice if he could be home Christmas.

The place we stayed last night was a nice place except that it was too hot there. This morning before we left, two Negro boys with a little monkey each came up to us and tried to sell them to us. They wanted $8.00 for them. We decided we didn't need one so we didn't get any. Also, we didn't have the money. I guess we get paid tomorrow.

I guess I will close for this time. Write me and I'll get the letter someday.

Love,
Odis

The final leg from South America was approximately 2,200 miles, all over water. It took over eleven and one-half hours to arrive at Dakar, Senegal, Africa. If there were problems with the planes on this leg, the crew would have to ditch their plane in the Atlantic Ocean, with little hope of survival. The B-24 was known to break in half upon ditching and would sink within seconds. Crew members could be severely injured or trapped in the tangle of the wreckage. The plane was equipped with survival gear such as life rafts, first-aid kits, flares, emergency rations, life preservers, etc.

The navigator did the initial navigation, with the radio operator locating a radio beam to follow approximately 200 miles from Dakar. Most crews landed with less than a half hour of fuel remaining, leaving a very little margin of safety. Some planes ran out of fuel on the runway just as they touched down.

Dakar, being the western most point of Africa and just north of the equator, was very hot and humid. The sleeping quarters and mess facilities were all in tents. Men had to sleep under mosquito nets for peace from the insects. The local natives were notorious for stealing, and everything had to be guarded, including the plane.

The fifth leg of the journey across the Sahara Desert was a seven hour flight of approximately 1400 miles to Marrakech, Morocco. The flight required a difficult crossing of the Atlas Mountains. The mountains were 14,000 feet high and the crew could not fly over 12,000 feet without oxygen, which was not supplied for the flight overseas. The only way through the mountains was a narrow pass at 8,000 feet. During this period, several planes crashed into the mountains. Only one plane from the 450th Bomb Group was lost in the mountains. The crews saw the first sign of war at Marrakech, where there was a large group of German prisoners of war held in confinement.

The briefing for the final leg informed them that the actual destination for the unit would be Italy, not England. The journey from Marrakech to Tunis, Tunisia, was approximately 1,000 miles and six hours flying time. Tunis was the crew's real introduction to the war. The ground was littered with burned out and shot-up trucks and all other types of military equipment, which was primarily German. The final battle in Africa that led to the defeat of Field Marshall Rommel in Africa was in the area of Tunis. The field was covered with bomb craters, and most of the hangars no longer had roofs. All manner of crashed and burned out aircraft littered the airfield.

Odis wrote his only letter from North Africa using the "V" mail system.

Sending letters by "V" mail was a unique way to save space, paper and labor. The letter to be sent was written on a page one quarter normal size. Numerous letters would be reduced to thumb-nail size on microfilm and sent back home where they were reproduced back to ? the normal size. A special envelope was used with a window showing the mailing address on the "V" mail. This system reduced what would previously require 37 mail bags down to one.

"V" mail envelope

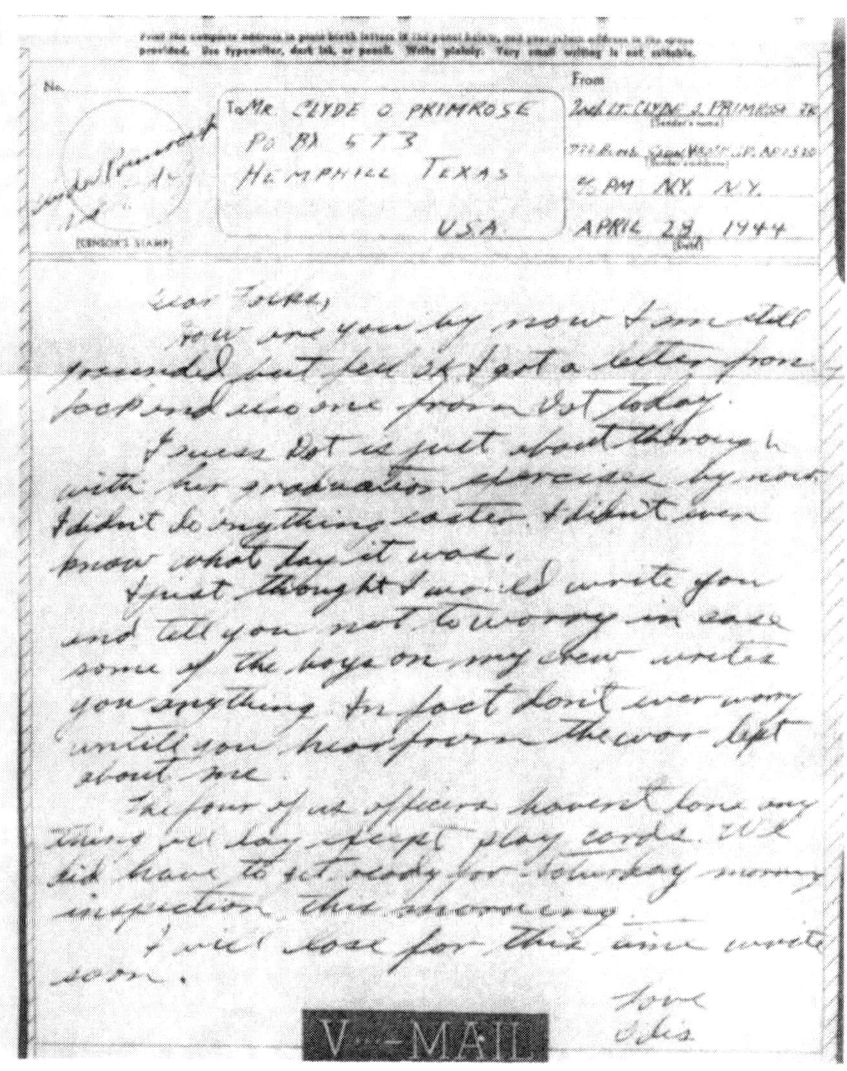

To MR. CLYDE O PRIMROSE
PO BX 573
HEMPHILL TEXAS
USA

From 2nd Lt. CLYDE A PRIMROSE JR.
(Sender's name)
(Sender's address)
% PM NY. N.Y.
APRIL 28, 1944
(Date)

(CENSOR'S STAMP)

Dear Folks,

How are you by now I am still grounded but feel ok. I got a letter from Jack and also one from Dot today.

I guess Dot is just about through with her graduation exercises by now. I didn't do anything easter. I didn't even know what day it was.

I just thought I would write you and tell you not to worry in case some of the boys on my crew writes you anything. In fact don't ever worry until you hear from the war dept about me.

The four of us officers haven't done any thing all day except play cards. We did have to get ready for Saturday morning inspection this morning.

I will close for this time write soon.

Love
[illegible]

V—MAIL

"V" mail letter (actual size)

January 15, 1944
Dear Folks,

How are you getting along by now? I am somewhere in Africa and am feeling fine. I am still on a vacation, but expect to catch up with our group soon. I am getting anxious to get to our destination and get some mail. If I can tell what I think I can, you will know what air force I'm in when I write you from my final destination. We won't be very far from the front lines and no water between us and the front lines.

Is Leon the same place he was? I will be a long distance from there. I would like for you to send me Jack's address if it has changed since I left. Well, I will close for this time. Don't worry if I don't write you often.

Love,
Odis

CHAPTER 13

Manduria, Italy

The flight from Tunis to Manduria, Italy was the final leg of the crew to the war zone. This was 500 miles and approximately 4 hours flying time over the colorful Mediterranean Sea. Their home was an old Italian fighter base with a 7000 ft dirt strip constructed in an olive grove. Due to the uneven surface and pot holes, the airfield was called "Lake Manduria" when it rained. The opposite occurred during the dry season when it became a dust bowl. This final stop was at the end of a 9,000 mile trip from the Continental U.S. (Author's note: I went through Manduria in 1977 and found it to be a nondescript town.)

The Ancient City of Manduria is located in the heel of the boot between the larger cities of Taranto and Lecce. The city was in existence under the Greek Empire. Hannibal conquered the city in 212 B.C., and used it for a watering station for his elephants during his invasion of the Roman Republic. After the Roman Empire fell, the city was invaded by many enemies until modern times, and has had a long history of both war and peace.

The 450th Bomb Group (heavy) was comprised of the 720th, 721st, 722nd, and the 723rd squadrons, and was one of 21 heavy bomb groups under the 15th Air Force. There were also seven fighter groups under the 15th.

The 15th was activated November 1, 1943, in Tunis, Tunisia, and then moved the headquarters to Bari, Italy, on December 1, 1943. Southern Italy was invaded after the fall of Sicily on September 3, 1942. On September 9, an allied force landed at Taranto, near Manduria, to sweep through the Italian heel and moved north to the middle of Italy. At the beginning of October, 1943, the Germans established a line across Italy north of Naples. The allied forces became bogged down on the Gustav line near Monte Cassino for the winter. The push through southern Italy left ample areas for the 15th Air Force to establish bases for each of the bomb groups.

The first plane of the 450 BG touched down at the Manduria Airfield in the rain on December 20, 1943. The field initially had one runway made of oiled clay and dirt with revetments on the sides for parking aircraft. Some areas had perforated steel planking (PSP), which is an ingenuous set of light weight interlocking panels that were put together on the ground, providing a hard surface for air strips or parking. During the rainy season there were very few high areas free from mud. The only living quarters available were old Italian barracks with no beds or cots. The crews only had what personal gear they brought in their duffle bags. The dirty barracks leaked when it rained, and had no heat or lights. Those who came in first found space in the barracks, and those following had to pitch tents in the mud.

The ground crew who came by ship, along with the major equipment and supplies, arrived the first part of January. The first ship arrived at the Port of Bari on New Years Eve. One of the other ships arrived at Naples and the final ship docked in Sicily on January 15, 1944. Since the ground crew arrived last, they had to put up G.I. two-man pup tents in the mud for their sleeping quarters. The German air raid on the Port of Bari sank and damaged some of their supply ships, increasing the discomfort of the men. As time progressed, the group received six-man pyramidal tents and floored them with salvaged packing crates.

The constant cold, along with the rain in January, made living conditions in tents and barracks miserable. The men made heaters, which consisted of 55 gallon drums placed horizontally on legs, with a stove pipe made from fuse cans welded together. Outside the tent or building, fuel tanks made from old oxygen tanks, or 55 gallon drums, were used to hold 100 octane gas for fuel. Fuel was fed by tubing from the gas to sand in the bottom of the heater drum, using a valve to control the flow. The fire was started using burning paper and drops of fuel. When a drop of fuel dropped to the sand it would vaporize and ignite, giving a continuous fire. This was the same type of system used by mess personnel to heat water for cooking and cleaning. As one might expect, some explosions happened and some fires were started.

The 450th group was faced with the monumental task of organizing the unit into a fighting force able to sustain the aircraft and administrative sections to accomplish their mission. Some materials and supplies became available from the Italian Navy in Taranto. Furniture from the now defunct Italian Air Force helped furnish offices. The group converted an old airplane hangar into the group headquarters. The unit had to set up mess halls, base aid station, briefing room, maintenance facilities, supply facilities, etc.

New improvements and small buildings were constructed out of tufa blocks. Tufa was a soft volcanic rock that was quarried locally. This material was used to build orderly and day rooms, and to block up sides of the tents. Plexiglass was added for windows. The base started taking shape with diesel generators providing lights to some of the facilities. Plumbing was added, along with heated showers. An outdoor screen was set up for movies. "Yankee" ingenuity was applied to all aspects of the base to provide as much comfort as possible.

The first Christmas overseas was somewhat bleak for the first crews that arrived on December 20, 1943. The military has always made every effort to have a special meal on Christmas; even if it meant packing a hot meal to the troops on the front lines. The men of the 450th received a first class traditional meal of turkey with all the trimmings, cranberry sauce, and pumpkin pie prepared by mess personnel in a tent under olive trees.

The base was never without something happening to keep things interesting. By the end of January the group was up to its full strength of 2,004 officers and enlisted men, making the base a beehive of activity. The base would be disturbed by air raid alerts, but seldom did the Germans venture into the area. British anti-aircraft crews provided protection. A few explosions of parked aircraft happened at night, and were attributed to sabotage. There were accidents with bombs and crashes on takeoffs and landings.

Manduria and other combat groups located in Southern Italy were able to bomb targets in Southern France, Southeastern Germany, Northern Italy, Austria, Yugoslavia, Czechoslovakia, Hungary, Bulgaria, Greece, and Romania. The Northwest portion of their range overlapped the range of the 8th Air Force out of England. The objective of the 15th Air Force was to destroy the German Air Force in the air and on the ground; concentrate on destruction of aircraft factories, ball bearing plants, refineries, ammunition plants, and sub pens; support the allies in battles on the Italian mainland and weaken the Germans in the Balkans.

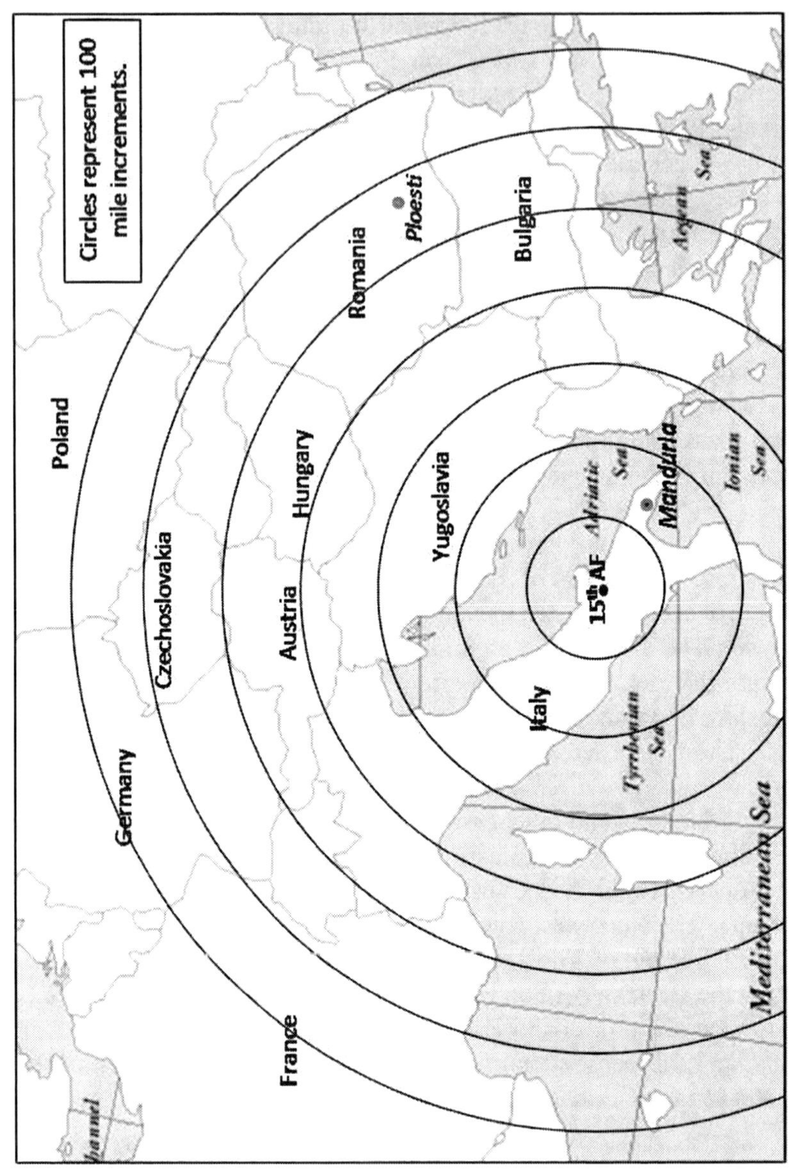

Area of operations for 450th BG

The 450th group came together as a fighting unit on January 8th when they made their first bomb run on the airdrome in Mostar, Yugoslavia. This was considered to be an easy "milk run" with little flak and no fighters encountered. The cloud cover made it questionable that the bombing was accurate.

Flight Officer Clyde Odis Primrose and his crew arrived in Manduria on January 31, 1944, after almost two months in transit, ready for combat.

Manduria Army Air Base
February 1, 1944

Dear Folks,

How are you by now? I am doing fine. We arrived here yesterday and I was really glad to get all of your letters. They were the first since I left New Mexico.

We had quite a trip coming over here. We stayed a few days everywhere we stopped and we saw lots of the country. We are some place in Italy and I think I am going to like it fine.

I imagine we will go on a mission tomorrow and see how we are going to like it. We have got to fly 50 missions before we can come home and most of the rest of the group are a few ahead of us. I don't think it is nearly as rough as I thought it was going to be. We haven't done anything in the past two months and its going to be hard to get back in the groove again.

I will try to write more often from now on. I hope to hear from you soon. I'll close for this time.

Love,
Odis

CHAPTER 14

What a Mission Is Like

Manduria Air base was far from an ideal base as compared to the comforts found on the U. S. bases. Equipment shortages were common in every area of operations. There had been very little change in the situation from December, 1943, until late spring. Some of the men were put in barracks which were run down and filthy. Others stayed in small six-man tents or two-man pup tents. Heating and hot water for showers was almost non-existent. In this early period, meals were prepared in tents, with most men eating while standing up outdoors. This deplorable situation was endured by crews who had to prepare for missions taking up to eight and one half hours.

Preparations for a mission started on the day before by checking the orderly room bulletin board to see if you were scheduled for a mission the next day. Generally, a crew would fly every other day. The plane assigned to you would not be listed until much later, depending on the status of repairs required after a previous mission. The original crews who came over from Alamogordo kept their planes for each mission, unless they required maintenance. When a crew had a day off, another crew might use their plane if needed by that squadron. The ground crews worked through most nights loading bombs, refueling, and making minor repairs. The bulk of their work was outdoors, regardless of the weather.

A long mission started with a wake-up call at 4:00 a.m. and a scheduled briefing at 6:00 a.m. Shorter missions would have a first call at 5:30 a.m. with a briefing at 7:00 a.m. Shaving in cold water became a routine thing. The crews had to be clean shaven to keep the oxygen mask from irritating the skin. They put on the warmest clothing they had, because the temperatures at high altitude could be as low as 50 degrees below zero. At that temperature, exposed skin would result in severe frost bite. Special flight clothing would be added prior to boarding the plane. The personal weapon for the crew was a .45 pistol in a shoulder holster. Each member had a set of "dog tags", which was their ID worn on a chain around their neck.

Breakfast was served in GI mess gear, which was a poor excuse for a food tray. Items such as eggs and potatoes were made from dehydrated stock, and had a taste unlike the original product. Toast, jelly, fruit, bacon, and coffee were available. After breakfast the main crew members split up and went to briefing that applied to individual jobs, such as, pilots, navigators, bombardiers, or radio operators. The gunners would depart for the plane to begin daily inspections and help with armament. A large map of the theater of operations would be uncovered showing the target for the mission to the pilots. Details would be covered; such as routes, rendezvous with other groups, fighter opposition, flak expected, and the route home.

After the briefing the crews would go to supply and pick up additional flying equipment: parachutes, escape kits, flak jackets, etc. Prior to boarding the plane the crew would put on light weight electrically heated suits and then sheepskin-lined leather flying suits. On top of all this bulging equipment came a Mae West life preserver, parachute harness, and a steel-plate lined flak jacket. The pilots wore back pack chutes, and the rest of the crew had chutes that would be attached to the harness if needed. Many times, as the crew prepared to board the aircraft, they would huddle together and someone would offer a prayer.

The crew had to struggle to get into position with the heavy equipment on, but more was to come. Since the majority of flying time was over 10,000 feet, oxygen was required to keep from losing consciousness. The plane had an oxygen system for crew members to plug into, and small short operation walk-around bottles were provided for moving around in the plane. The oxygen masks fit very tightly on the face, causing discomfort. A head set and a throat microphone for communications added to the discomfort. Some men took tasteless "K" rations for snacks. However, the below freezing temperatures caused everything to freeze. After all the equipment was on, the pilot and co-pilot went through the take off check list.

The first danger on a mission came on start-ups and take-offs. Engines were started by power from small internal gas powered units with the danger of igniting fuel vapors. As the planes prepared for take off, a green flare would signal to start the mission, and a red flare would signal to abort the mission for reasons such as a sudden change in weather. After start-up and moving into position, the planes would take off at 30 to 60 second intervals leaving no room for error or problems. To take off 20-25 tons of steel, aluminum, fuel, people, and bombs had to move down a short runway while gaining a speed close to 120 miles per hour to become airborne. On several occasions, a plane would fail to lift off the runway and would crash at the end of the runway, with succeeding planes flying through the smoke and debris.

The next element of danger was the 35 to 40 minutes of circling the field waiting for everyone to take off and form a group formation. The possibility was great for mid-air collisions. There would be 30 to 42 planes taking part in a maximum mission, depending on aircraft availability. The group then advanced to mate up with other groups of the 15th AF to complete the task force for the mission. Some missions had all four groups of the 47th wing, and special large missions could have over 20 groups with the addition of the 5th, 55th, 49th and 304th wing aircraft. At some point after assembling the group and joining other groups, the gunners would test fire their .50 cal. machine guns to insure they were functioning correctly. Flying with numerous groups created congestion in the air. Prop wash from other aircraft caused sudden movements resulting in some collisions. The B-24 was a difficult plane to hold in a tight formation.

The first task for pilots after the group began to assemble was to get into a formation called the "combat box" to provide for maximum defense against fighters. A box would contain up to 21 planes staggered vertically and horizontally. Each staggered segment would have six to seven aircraft in the shape of a "V". A front view would show each segment one under the other. On large missions with several groups, there would be several boxes behind each other.

The front plane of a single or several groups was the lead aircraft. The other planes followed it to the target and dropped bombs at the same time as the lead plane. One aircraft was designated deputy lead, in case the lead plane was hit by fighters or flak.

The second hour of flying at high altitude in very tight formation caused the pilot and co-pilot to have aching hands, arms, legs, and backs. They did swap-off flying the aircraft when possible. The rest of the crew was also physically and mentally tired. Usually by the third hour, fighters would start to arrive, keeping the gunners alert and busy. The German Focke-Wulf 190 and Messerschmitt 109 fighters were armed with 20mm cannons and 13mm machine guns. The 20mm shell would explode on contact and send shrapnel through the plane, cutting lines, starting fires, and wounding or killing crew members. Bullets and canon shells from the fighters would rattle through the plane after a pass. If a crew member was wounded, very little blood would show due to the freezing conditions, which caused the blood to congeal. Crew members used their "walk around" oxygen bottles when they left their post to assist the wounded crew members.

When the flight neared the target, the fighters dropped out and the anti-aircraft fire, called "flak", began. The word "flak" was a contraction of a German word meaning anti-aircraft weapon. The 88mm was the most common and most accurate flak gun used. It had a 20 lb. projectile with a range of just over 26,000 ft. The Germans also had some larger guns of 105 mm. The fuse was set prior to firing and timed to go off at the elevation of the flight. The German crews were very proficient gunners. The black clouds of flak bursts were so numerous that crew members said it looked like they could walk on them.

The flak shell would go off with a red flash, surrounded by a black puff of smoke. The 88 mm burst had a lethal range of 30 ft., destroying any plane within that distance. Flak is hot enough to start fires at close range. At ranges beyond 30 ft. the fragments caused serious-to-fatal wounds along with cutting fuel, oxygen, hydraulic lines, and damaging wiring and control cables. The sound of flak hitting the plane sounded like rocks rolling around in a tin can. It was not unusual to find over 100 holes in the skin of a plane at the end of a mission. The only defense used against flak was to drop bundles of shredded aluminum foil, called "chaff", or "window". These small particles floating down would be picked up by ground radar making it difficult for the operators to locate the exact position of the planes.

When the formation was near the starting point of the bomb run (called I.P. or Initial Point), the crew would put on their steel helmets and flak jackets, as the anti-aircraft fire would begin. The lead bombardier would take control of the plane soon after the I.P., using the bomb sight in conjunction with the auto-pilot, to determine when the bombs are to be released on the target. This is a very simplified explanation of a very detailed set of adjustments the bombardier had to make to the bomb sight for it to compute the release point. He also set what was called an intervalometer for the bombs to fall in a pattern that would string them over the target. When the lead aircraft dropped their bombs, it was a signal for the planes behind to release theirs. This method was called "toggling" the bombs, since the bomb sight was not used by anyone other than the lead plane. During the final bomb run, the planes had to fly straight and level, giving the flak gunners perfect targets. No evasive action could be taken during the bomb run.

A direct hit from flak could be a devastating experience to a crew, and very few members would survive. For example, in the mission to Ploesti on July 15th by the 98th Bomb Group, a B-24H aircraft number 42-95463 took a direct hit in the nose of the plane blowing the nose section off up to the windshield. The three crew members, bombardier, navigator, and the nose gunner were blown away with parts of the nose and did not survive. The co-pilot, Bob Dean, in a letter dated March, 5, 2001 indicated four crew members got out the bomb bay, and the fifth went out the waist window. The right and left waist gunners, along with the tail gunner, were trapped by centrifugal force and went down with the plane. Dean also stated that when the plane was hit in the nose by the flak, it went out of control and was on fire as it started going down. The bodies of the navigator and the bombardier were seen by the radioman in a German aid station after capture. (Author's note: There will be more about July 15, 1944 in Chapter 16.)

The return trip back to base was somewhat a repeat of the first half of the mission. After bomb release the plane was still in range of flak guns. As soon as they left the general target area, the fighters would again attack while over the enemy territory, and would concentrate on any planes that were dropping out of formation due to flak damage. Planes suffering severe frame or engine damage, or fuel loss, had to be abandoned or alternate landing sites had to be found. Crews going down over the Mediterranean or Adriatic seas were faced with serious decisions. A plane with wounded on board would have to make a crash landing or ditch in the sea, if the wounded could not bail out. The B-24 was noted for breaking in half when it hit the water, with heavy loss of life. Parachuting over open water was not without hazards, as the crew would be spread out over a large area, with only life preservers to keep them afloat. Their only chance for survival was to radio ahead, with the hope that the sea rescue crews would make it before hypothermia set in.

One of the 450th planes with wounded on board came back to the field with severe damage to the hydraulics and the lifting mechanism of the belly turret (ball turret). When the plane came in for a crash landing, the belly turret gunner was killed instantly, since there was no way to lift him back inside the plane.

The return to base was a relief from long hours of the living hell; being shot at by fighters, enduring flak, and seeing some of your comrades killed or wounded. A plane with heavy damage or wounded on board would shoot a red flare into the air signaling a problem, and was given priority to land. Fire fighting equipment and ambulances would be prepared to meet them. After landing, a report of damage or equipment problems would be made out for the maintenance crews, so that they could start working to prepare the plane for the next mission. The crews would be met by a Red Cross crew handing out coffee and doughnuts. The flight surgeon would also pass out a small quantity of whiskey to each crew member to hopefully calm their nerves.

The final chore after the mission was the debriefing of the crew. Crews would go to their respective areas for extensive interrogation about every aspect of the mission. Information was recorded on strike estimates, flak encountered, and fighter strength. Crew members were questioned about parachutes seen and the damage and the identity of planes that went down.

It has been stated that of the 62 crews that left Alamogordo, only about 12 returned to the states. This did not include complete original crews since some individual members substituted on other crews and were killed. It is estimated that probably only two or three complete crews returned. The 450th BG served for sixteen months and had a loss of over 1500 men killed or missing in action. During this period, the 15th Air Force lost 2,380 planes out of 4,951 assigned to them for a loss of 48 percent.

CHAPTER 15

Combat

The 15th Air Force was activated on November 1, 1943, in Tunis, Tunisia, and relocated to Bari, Italy, on December 1, 1943, with initial groups transferred from the 8th Air Force in England. The 450th BG was the first of the new groups in Italy to arrive from the states. The first aircraft landed on December 20, 1943. The unit became operational the first of January, with the first mission on January 8 to the airdrome at Mostar, Yugoslavia. In January of 1944, the Germans were only 350 miles north of Manduria and just south of Rome. Occasionally, they would send a bomber south to bomb the base, but did almost no damage.

Flight Officer Clyde Odis Primrose arrived in Manduria, Italy, on January 31, 1944, and wrote his first letter from the combat zone. Two days later he went on his first mission to the marshaling yards (rail yards) at Pontassieve, Italy. Thirty-five planes left with twelve 500 lb bombs each, with three planes returning early. Planes would return early due to mechanical problems or serious injuries from fighter attacks.

Manduria, Italy
February 2, 1944

Dear Folks,

How are you by now? I am feeling fine. I went on my first mission today and I know how it feels to be shot at. I received two letters from you today. One was written on the 14th and one on the 12th.

I think I am going to like it fine over here after we finally get straightened out. It's pretty cold here, but I guess it will warm up soon.

I guess it's a good thing Jack isn't going to go in the cadets. I think it would be a good deal if he could get in, but I'm sure he couldn't pass the physical.

I am glad you had a nice Christmas and I hope to be home for the next.

I will write every chance I get and I hope you don't worry about me too much and I want you to write me real often.

Love,
Odis

On February 8, Odis made a mission to the main Airdrome in Viterbo, Italy, and dropped one ton of incendiary bombs.

February 8, 1944

Dear Folks,

How are you by now? I am 21 years old today and am feeling fine. In case you didn't get my other letter, I'm still in Italy.

We went on a raid today and I'm pretty tired. I have a few blisters on my hands from flying in formation. Combat is not as rough as I had it pictured, but it's rough enough. You really feel better after you have dropped your bombs on the target and started home. Just before you get to the target, you wonder what is going to happen. The Red Cross is doing a good job over here. They have hot coffee and doughnuts and we really do appreciate them. The medical department issues out a shot of whiskey to each man when he comes back off a mission, but so far I have not wanted more.

I just received three letters from you and I got one from Harold the other day. I'm glad you are getting along ok and hope you will continue to do so.

Hoping to hear from you soon, I will close for this time.

Love,
Odis

February 10, 1944

Dear Folks,

How are you by now? I am ok. I received three letters from you last night. Of course they were pretty old, but I was glad to get them. There has not been anything out of your letters and as far as I know, none of them have been censored. There's not a thing I can tell you about what I am doing here concerning combat missions or give any names of towns around here. I can't say anything about loss of life or crack ups.

We went into town yesterday and bought some cheese, almond candy, shelled almonds and some eggs. All of which was very high. Eggs were 10 cents each. We came back and fried them on a little hot plate we paid $10 for, and all four of us were sick this morning.

I hope you can get the house fixed up ok. I wish I could send you more money, but when I make 2nd Lt. I will make $22.00 less than what I'm making now. I am making almost what a 1st Lt. does now, but I have to make 2nd Lt. before I can go any higher.

Love,
Odis

On February 16, Odis made a second mission to the marshaling yards in Pontassieve, Italy with a bomb load of three tons.

On February 17th, Odis flew on a mission with 3 tons of 500 lb. bombs to bomb the German stores behind the lines to support the Anzio beachhead. The allied forces had landed at Salerno on the mainland of Italy in September, and were still stalemated around Cassino by January. A landing north of Cassino on January 22 at Anzio, fifty miles from Rome, was designed to outflank the Germans at Cassino and cut off their retreat north. This was a hasty and ill conceived plan which split the allied forces at Cassino and failed to cause the Germans to retreat. The Germans conducted a massive counter attack on February 16, designed to push the invaders back into the sea at Anzio. The counter attack by the Germans, along with another one, failed, but the German forces kept the invading force on the beachhead under constant fire for almost three months. The 15th Air Force was called upon numerous times to support the Anzio landing and the stalemate at Cassino.

Friday
February 18, 1944

Dear Folks,

How are you by now? I am ok. I received your letter yesterday that you wrote on the 22nd of January and I'm as far away from that as I can be and still be on the same piece of land.

We don't know anything about what is going on over here except what we do. Some of the fellows have radios, but I never get around to listening to any news.

It hasn't been too rough so far over here, but you can see that we will pull some real tough raids after we get a little experience and that's not far off. We made a pass through a flack alley yesterday.

I haven't met any girls around here and I don't think I will. There's not many here and they are no good. The people are ok around here, but most of them are very poor. We have a couple of Italian soldiers for orderlies in our barracks. They are still in the army, but I don't think they get anything but what they eat and I don't know who pays for that.

If you read any news about our A.F. you will know I'm in it. Have you read much news about the 15th?

I'll close for this time. Write every chance you get.

Love,
Odis

The raid that Odis made on Thursday, the 17th was on the Anzio Beachhead that was defended by heavy, intense and very accurate flak. The bombing was accurate, destroying German stores of supplies.

The week of February 22, 1944, became known as "Big Week" due to the combined efforts of the 8th Air Force in England and the 15th Air Force in Italy to make massive bombing strikes deep into Germany. The main objective was to hit the German Aircraft Industry in order to reduce the number of planes available to intercept allied bombers. The objective achieved limited success, but with a high cost in the loss of over 225 bombers and their crews.

On February 23, Odis participated in the raid on the Aero Engine Works in Steyr, Austria, where four bombers were lost to fighters and three others were missing. On February 25, Odis again flew a mission deep into Germany to drop 1000 lb bombs on the Prufening Aircraft Factory in Regensburg, Germany, which produced ME109 fighters. The bombers were attacked twice by fighters in route to the target and encountered heavy flak. The mission was so successful that the 450th was awarded a unit citation for outstanding performance of duty in armed conflict with the enemy. Lt. Col. Robert Gideon, the group leader, was awarded a Silver Star and each crew member received a letter of commendation for their part in the mission. (More about Lt. Col. Gideon in the Epilogue)

Friday
February 25, 1944

Dear Folks,

How are you by now? I am well and doing fine. I hope you all are the same. I am pretty tired tonight. I went on a mission today that you will probably read about tomorrow. I can't tell you much about what I am doing, but if you read the papers you will know. I have been on quite a few missions and I have seen a lot of the things you read about in the papers. There has never been a fighter dive directly at my ship (I'm happy to say), but I have seen them when they meant business. I get to see all the action because my first pilot always flies the ship when we get into trouble. Everything is up to snuff so far.

I hated to hear that Jess Jr. washed out, but everybody who tries for the cadets does not make the grade. I was just lucky, I guess.

Your mail is not censored, so ask me all the questions you want and I will try to answer them.

Don't worry about me and write often.

Love,
Odis

The twin tails of the 450th B-24s had the rudders painted white. The remainder of the tail section had two white circles for the identification of the 47th Wing and group. The markings allowed unit identification in the air when numerous groups flew together on large missions. During "Big Week," the German Luftwaffe recognized the 450th by these white rudders and by the accuracy of their bombing. The German propaganda radio broadcast by "Axis Sally," on February 26 said, "The Luftwaffe will be waiting for the white tail Liberators from Southern Italy." Shortly after that broadcast, the 450th became known as the "Cottontails." In April, all of the tail sections were re-painted with a design the German pilots could not recognize as easily from the air, with the hope they would not be singled out.

March 1, 1944

Dear Folks,

How are you by now? I am ok. I received a letter from you yesterday with Jack's address, but couldn't make out part of it, but I suppose he will write me in a few days.

I am going to send some money for Dot's graduation present. She can use it for whatever she needs.

I have quite a collection of different kinds of money. I got some in about every place I stayed. I don't have so many coins because most places have all paper money. I don't have any Italian money, but I ought to get some before I leave here.

Well, I have been here a month and didn't quite get the number of missions I have to get every month. My goal is to be ready to come home by the end of June. Of course it will take a month or more after I get my missions in to get home.

I can't think of anything to write, so guess I will have to close. Answer soon.

Love,
Odis

Sunday
March 5, 1944

Dear Folks,

How are you by now? I am ok. I just got a letter from you tonight and was very glad to hear from you and can't understand why you have not heard from me yet.

I guess the puppies are getting pretty big by now. I hope they make good squirrel dogs. I hope to be home some time this fall or winter and go squirrel hunting. I should be home if I get my 50 missions in this theater, by September or October. Of course I have a long way to go yet. I haven't done a thing all day except go to church.

I got paid today and I am going to send a little for Dot's expenses tomorrow. We had to donate $5.00 more to our squadron mess and $5.00 more to the group's officers club this month. We have the best officer's mess in the group and I think the officer's club is going to be pretty nice when they get it finished. It cost lots of money to fix up anything like that. I don't expect we will have much time to spend in the club as soon as we start having good weather.

I hear from Jack pretty often. I know he must be pretty homesick by now. He's been in the army almost a year hasn't he? In letters he wrote to me, he seemed to like the new outfit he is in. It seems like a good deal to me. I don't expect he will be sent to this theater and if he is he will be as safe as if he were at home.

Well, as I have no news, I'll close for this time. Write me often.

Love,
Odis

Odis flew a mission on March 7 to the marshalling yards in Cartaldo, Italy, with 500 lb bombs. The group did not encounter any fighters or flak on the mission. The group flew a mission to the submarine pens at Toulon, France, on March 11, but Odis and his crew were off that day, except one man. Probably because his letters were being censored, he could not explain things the way he normally would, making his letter on March 11 somewhat confusing. He talked about one crew member that substituted with another crew using their normal plane "Janner." His indication is this crew member had been sick so he was substituting on his day off to catch up on missions.

Saturday
March 11, 1944

Dear Folks,

How are you by now? I am ok. and feeling fine. I received two letters from you, one from Dot and one from Dad.

I sent $50 to you for Dot, but I don't know when you will get it.

Yes, I am still a Flight Officer, but I get almost as much money as a 1st Lt. does over here. Our C.O. called us all in the other day and told us that it might be 4 or 5 months before we get 2nd Lt. and he would try to get 1st for us within a couple of months after that. It seems that every time they get the papers fixed up on us Flight Officers and get them up to the 15th A.F. the ruling has changed and they send them back. They have come back 3 times since I have been over here. I guess the most I can hope for over here is 1st Lt and be lucky to get that.

I am still flying with the same crew except number 3 on top row of picture. We have been lucky. We only got a few holes in our ship. Of course we don't fly our ship every time. I have never had to substitute on any other crew. I was talking about the picture with the caps off. He didn't get to fly much when we got over here because of a bad cold. The one under the "J" in some picture had some trouble, but he flew today in our ship with another crew.

I really got that last paragraph messed up, didn't I? I was going to tell you something that we weren't allowed to and finally gave up the idea. Well, anyway, if anything happens in this area, you can bet I'm in on it.

Well, I have got this letter messed up so I guess I will quit until next time. Write often and tell me the news. Also, let me know anytime my mail is censored or cut up.

Love,
Odis

P.S. Is Leon still a Captain?

The crew member in the picture mentioned by Odis was identified as Staff Sergeant James M. Reese. Odis was about to say he was lost on that day, but realized the censors would not allow it, so he changed the subject. On March 11th, Staff Sergeant Reese was flying in the original plane that Odis and his crew came over in from the states, but not with its original crew. Many times when a crew had a day off, their plane would be used by another crew in order to have sufficient planes for a mission. Many returning planes would be out of service due to damage.

The mission that day was with 36 B-24s loaded with 1000 lb bombs. German fighters attacked the formations in large numbers bringing down "Janner," Odis' original plane. Staff Sergeant Reese was in that plane. The plane was attacked and shot down by an unusual plane. It was a captured British Spitfire with German markings. An eye witness from a tail gunner in the same formation reported seeing "Janner" piloted by 2nd Lt. Frank Brusek hit and falling out of formation with fire in the wing. Seconds afterward, the plane blew up, falling into the sea with no parachutes seen. On the same mission, another B-24 crashed near shore and ten unidentified bodies were recovered and buried by the Germans. Originally, their bodies were thought to be those of "Janner." A later investigation in November indicated that the remains were that of a 1st Lt. Vail and his crew that had gone down that same day. Nothing was ever recovered from "Janner," since it exploded and fell into the sea.

Staff Sergeant James Reese was a married man from Chambersburg, Pennsylvania, who had enlisted in January, 1943. Since he was lost at sea, his name appears at the Rhone American Cemetery in Draguignan, France. A memorial marker for Reese is also located at the Gettysburg National Military Park in Gettysburg, Pa.

Thursday
March 16, 1944

Dear Folks,

How are you by now? I am feeling fine and was lucky and didn't get caught in the snow. I got a letter from Jack yesterday. I am getting plenty of sleep. I woke up this morning and heard it raining outside and turned over and went back to sleep. I finally got up about eleven o'clock.

Well, I guess you do a lot of worrying whether I get back from these missions or not. There's no use for you to worry when you read something in the papers, because I don't go on every mission and we only lose a small percent. I am still with the same crew and I have one of the best pilots in the group. When we get a plane of our own so that we can keep all the little odds and ends in good shape, I think we will make it ok.

We have our mess hall fixed up a little better now. We covered our tables with ply board today. We may not have food as good as we would in the states, but at least we don't have to eat out of mess kits. The enlisted men still have to eat out of mess kits, but I think they will get their mess hall fixed up pretty soon.

Have you heard any news on how Philip, J.B. Walker and Brown are making out in the cadets? I hear they are washing the cadets out for almost anything these days. I know they will feel pretty bad if they don't make it after an old country boy like myself made it.

Well, I hope you all get along o.k. and I hope you got the $50 I sent Dot for graduation expenses. I will close for this time. Write often and don't worry about me.

Love,
Odis

On April 2, Odis went on a mission to the Daimler-Puch Factory in Steyr, Austria, along with 41 other bombers loaded with 500 lb bombs. The group received heavy damage from fighters and flak. On April 5, Odis participated in a historic raid on the oil center in Ploesti, Romania, for which the 450th received its second unit citation. This was the first attack on the oil center in Ploesti in 1944 by the 450th and over seven months since the disastrous raid from North Africa in August, 1943. The mission encountered a heavy fighter concentration and very heavy flak. The Germans had developed a very sophisticated system using smoke to cover the target area making precise bombing very difficult.

The pilot, 1st Lt. Frank Marpe of the deputy lead aircraft received the Distinguished Service Cross for his heroism on that mission. The crew had forgotten two parachutes when they had to transfer to another plane at the last minute due to an oil leak. Lt. Marpe gave his parachute to another crewman and planned to jump double with another crew member. The plane was near the target when it was hit by fighters. That started a fuel and oxygen fire in the bomb bay, and seconds later, the plane exploded. Lt. Marpe stayed with the plane to hold it level to give his crew a chance to bail out. He went down in flames with the plane. Only two crew members made it out of the plane.

The mission was conducted at 23,000 ft. altitude which caused Odis to have a severe ear problem which gave him trouble from that date on. The bombardier, Lt. Walker, also suffered from the same problem. This mission was in their new airplane which they named "Janner II." The new plane, #216, was received the last of March. It was shot down over Ploesti Romania on June 26, with a different crew on board.

Tuesday
April 11, 1944

Dear Folks,

How are you by now? I am in the hospital now having a little ear trouble, but I expect to get out about the last of the week. I came in here last Thursday and haven't felt like writing up until now.

I can't tell you any of the missions that I have been on, but I have been on most of the important ones out of this area. We have our own ship now, but we haven't painted the name on it yet. We are going to call it "Janner II." Well, my score is 19 now. We are having some nice weather here now and I'm in the hospital. I guess the rest of my crew will get way ahead of me. Walker, our bombardier was in the hospital all last week and is supposed to start back flying tomorrow. He is quite a bit behind the rest of us.

Well, I finally made 2nd Lt. The adjutant came over and swore me in yesterday. We aren't going to get a reduction in pay anyway. When I make 1st, if I ever do, I'll only get a $5.00 raise. When I get back to the States and don't get overseas pay it will make quite a bit of difference.

We are getting replacements all the time and maybe Don Easley's boy will be sent to my outfit. They are working up a new deal on the fellows that get 50 missions in. They send them home for a month and then right back to their old outfit. Well, I hope I get to spend more than a month in the states when I get back.

Well, I guess I will close for this time. I hope Billy Boy and all of you are getting along ok. Write soon.

Love,
Odis

Friday
April 21, 1944

Dear Folks,

How are you by now? I receive two letters from you today and am glad that Billy is getting along ok. I got out of the hospital today, but I still don't feel too well. I also got a letter from Jack today. By the way, S. T. wrote me a letter here awhile back and didn't put a return address on it, so I couldn't answer it.

We have been having some real nice weather all this month and I missed all the good flying weather, except the final three or four days of the month. I guess I'll be able to start back to flying in about a week. Our crew is due to go to rest camp sometime in the near future, but the date hasn't been set.

Have you heard any news lately on Booley and Westley coming home? Do you think Booley is going to marry his girl in England?

I got a commendation on the Regensburg raid I was on and I am sending it along with this letter. I have already earned the Air medal and two Oak Leaf clusters and maybe I'll get some more before I get back home, but I hope I don't get the Purple Heart.

Well, I'm pretty tired, so I guess I will close for tonight. Answer soon.

Love,
Odis

Odis' uncle, Booley did marry the girl from England, brought her to the states, and raised a family of two girls and four boys.

722ND BOMBARDMENT SQUADRON (H) AAF
450TH BOMBARDMENT GROUP (H) AAF
OFFICE OF THE COMMANDING OFFICER
APO 520 US ARMY

19 APRIL 1944

SUBJECT: COMMENDATION FOR PARTICIPATING IN THE REGENSBURG, GERMANY RAID OF 25 FEBRUARY 1944.

TO: 2ND LT. CLYDE [illegible]

1. YOU ARE TO BE HIGHLY COMMENDED FOR THE PART YOU PLAYED IN THE HIGHLY SUCCESSFUL RAID ON REGENSBURG, GERMANY FLOWN ON 25 FEBRUARY 1944.

2. THIS RAID WAS CONDUCTED UNDER EXTREMELY ADVERSE CONDITIONS AND THE FOLLOWING MEDALS WERE AWARDED:

GROUP LEADER, LT. COL. ROBERT R. GIDEON -- (SILVER STAR)

LEAD BOMBARDIER, 1ST LT. ROLLAND R. CARR -- (DISTINGUISHED FLYING CROSS)

LEAD NAVIGATOR, 1ST LT. ROBERT L. BROWN -- (DISTINGUISHED FLYING CROSS)

3. A COPY OF THIS LETTER HAS BEEN PLACED IN YOUR 201 FILE.

4. BY YOUR DEVOTION TO YOUR COUNTRY AND ATTENTION TO DUTY YOU HAVE REFLECTED GREAT CREDIT ON THE 450TH BOMBARDMENT GROUP AND THE 722ND BOMBARDMENT SQUADRON.

John S. Mills
JOHN S. MILLS,
COLONEL, AIR CORPS
GROUP COMMANDER

William L. Orris
WILLIAM L. ORRIS,
MAJOR, AIR CORPS
SQUADRON COMMANDER

-1-

Commendation for Regensburg raid.

Wednesday
April 26, 1944

Dear Folks,

How are you by now? I am feeling pretty good but I'm still grounded. I received two V-mail letters from you today. One was written on the 9th and one on the 12th of April and was very glad to get them. I guess you have just about learned to not worry when you don't hear from me. I think it takes my mail longer to get to you than it does for yours to get over here. I hear from Jack pretty regularly.

Well, I know Westley is really glad to get back. I sure would like to see him. Have you heard from Booley lately?

My crew is quite a few missions ahead of me now. I only have 19 and I'm hoping to get in a few more before we go to rest camp. On one of the missions the crew went on a 20mm came in the side of the ship and exploded, but no damage was done. One of the waist gunners got a small scratch on the hand. I don't mind the 20mm or rockets much, but when those 109s come in they don't care how close they get, I don't believe. When they get in close enough and lined up on you they cut loose and it looks like both of his wings are on fire and they are in and out in about 10 seconds. I get a big kick out of this combat, but I do get pretty scared sometimes. We have a little guy on our crew (radio man) and it makes him mad when fighters start coming in on us. He never gets excited; he just cusses them and lets them have it. He is the best enlisted man on our crew. We lost two of our enlisted men. One went back to the states and I don't know where the other one is.

I don't know why you didn't get a bond this month. They took it out of my pay.

I hated to hear about James B and Philip. I guess they think they got a raw deal and they might have.

Well, I have run out of anything to write about, so I will close for tonight. Write every chance you get.

Love,
Odis

April 28, 1944

Dear Folks,

How are you by now? I am still grounded, but feel ok. I got a letter from Jack and one from Dot today.

I guess Dot is just about through with her graduation exercises by now.

I didn't do anything Easter; I didn't even know what day it was.

I just thought I would write you and tell you not to worry in case some of the boys on my crew write you anything. In fact, don't ever worry until you hear from the war department about me.

The four of us officers haven't done anything all day except play cards. We did have to get ready for Saturday morning inspection this morning.

I will close for this time. Write soon.

Love,
Odis

Odis and officers of "Janner" at Manduria.

On April 29, the 450th carried out a raid on the Harbor Installations at Toulon, France, and lost three aircraft over the target area. One of the planes that went down was the lead group plane piloted by Major Orris, the Squadron Commander of the 722nd, with a hand picked crew, including the squadron navigator and bombardier. The remaining four original enlisted crew members of Odis' plane, A. J. Kosak, Albert Slinkard, Lowell Root, and Melvin Fouer, were picked to finish out the crew. The plane was hit by flak during the bomb run and smoke was coming out of the waist section when orders were given to bail out. All ten of the crew members bailed out with only minor injuries. However, they were captured by the Germans and sent to Dulag Luft in Frankfort, Germany, for interrogation. After interrogation, officers were sent to Stalag Luft III at Sagan, Germany, and the enlisted men went to Stalag Luft IV. The Russians, advanced west and caused the Germans to force march all allied prisoners of war westward, with many of the weaker ones dying in the sub zero weather. Major Orris was able to escape and hide in the woods for two weeks until the Americans came through. All four of Odis' crew survived the march and were liberated at Stalag 17B. The July, 1945, issue of the National Geographic had a story about Major Orris and his life as a POW.

The Toulon mission also claimed the plane piloted by 2nd Lt. Maddux, when flak hit in the #3 engine setting it on fire. Eight crew members parachuted out. One drowned in the harbor, but the others were rescued. The tail gunner and the left waist gunner went down with the plane.

On May 5th, Odis had been returned to flying status and made his second mission to Ploesti to bomb the marshalling yards. Each plane carried ten 500 lb bombs. No letters arrived during the month of May, but he accumulated credit for 15 missions giving him a total of 34.

At home during this time, changes were being made in the Primrose household. Odis' oldest sister, Dorothy, graduated from high school at the age of 17 in the spring of 1944. Even with all the manufacturing throughout the country, none of the work found its way to deep East Texas. There was no work for a young girl just out of high school in Hemphill. Dot moved to Ballinger, Texas, to live with and work for kinfolks. Dot was missed greatly. She worked hard while at home, either in the fields or in the house. Many times she did the cooking and took care of the little ones while her mom was doing other work on the farm. She was like a second mother to the younger kids.

After Dot left, Leatrice was the oldest at home, and took command of the younger kids. She was a hard worker and expected the others to be the same. Faye and Frances gave her the most trouble. They were mischievous, and were jokingly called the "Katzenjammer Kids." She got her bluff in on Shirley, Dixie, and Mary Jane, so they fell quickly in line. Bill was a baby at that time.

Odis spent a week at rest camp the last of May and first of June. Most crews went to the Isle of Capri or Naples after completing half of their missions, for a much deserved break from combat flying.

Tuesday
June 6, 1944

Dear Folks,

How are you by now? I am doing ok. I just got back from rest camp and am ready to start to work on the 16 missions I lack. I really enjoyed my stay at rest camp. We stayed in a nice hotel with soft beds with sheets and pillows. We had steak every day and eggs for breakfast anyway we wanted them cooked. The hotel was right on the edge of the sea and we could go sail boat riding or swimming. I never got up enough energy to do either.

Has Westley gone back or is he going back? I didn't know that they could send anybody back so quick. I haven't heard from Jack since he got over, but I'll sure try to locate him if he comes to Italy.

Well, I never have any news and I always hate to sit down to write. I will close for tonight.

Love,
Odis

Tuesday
June 12, 1944

Dear Folks,

How are you by now? I am up and feeling fine, but I haven't been on a mission since I got back from rest camp. Mac and Decker have 48 missions each, Walker has 41 and I only have 34. They have been flying new fellows with Mac and I am way behind. I think maybe I will have a crew of my own after Mac finishes.

It's really getting hot over here now and I can't get to sleep until about 11:00 or 12:00 p.m. I don't know what I will do when I start back to flying and they come in and wake me up at 2:45 a.m. and I have had only 3 hours of sleep.

Well, as I have no news, I will close. Write often.

Love,
Odis

Most of the original crews from Alamogordo, who survived combat, finish the required 50 missions by the first of June. Those who were sick or spent time in the hospital recovering from wounds were behind the regular crew members. The pilot of Lt. Primrose's group, John McLaughlin completed his 50 missions, was promoted to captain, and became the Group Operations Officer.

Monday
June 19, 1944

Dear Folks,

How are you by now? I am doing ok. I received two letters from you yesterday and three from Jack day before yesterday. He seems to like it pretty well in England and he should be pretty safe there. The ground personnel here are worrying about when they will get home and we are worrying about getting home.

I have had a pretty easy time of it the last month. I have only been on one mission this month and we had no flak and no fighters on that one. Mac and Decker are all finished and Walker has 6 to go and I have 15 to go. I don't know whether I am going to get checked out or not. I would rather have a crew of my own than to be put with a new replacement crew. If I get a crew, I will have a good chance of making 1st Lt, before I come home.

The war situation looks pretty good over here, but it's going to take a little time to hem them up.

We are having some hot and dry weather over here now. It hasn't rained enough to count in the last month and a half.

I don't have any news so I will close for this time. Write every chance you get.

Love,
Odis

The mission Odis mentioned in the above letter was made to Osijck, Yugoslavia oil refinery on June 14. No fighters or flak were encountered.

Friday
June 23, 1944

Dear Folks,

How does this letter find you? I am doing ok. I still haven't flown any more missions, but I know I will soon. I received a letter from you today that was written on the 9th.

I have been to almost all those places you mentioned and some of them more than once. You don't have to worry about me. Even if I get shot down I have a good chance of coming out of it ok. I have seen plenty parachutes.

The air medals are given to all men who fly 10 combat missions and you get an oak leaf cluster for every 10 after that. Also clusters are given for other things. If you get wounded, you get the Purple Heart.

We are having some hot weather over here and the wind blows most of the time, so we have to put up with a lot of dust.

Well, as there is no news I will close. Write every chance you get.

Love,
Odis

P. S. I think I have been getting all of your letters.

Tuesday,
July 4, 1944

Dear Folks,

How are you by now? I am ok. I just thought I would write you a few lines to let you know I'm ok.

I haven't flown any more missions, but I guess I will pretty soon. I have just been taking it easy and I don't intend to get in a hurry to finish my missions.

It is really hot over here these days and the dust has really been bad here today.

I got a couple of letters from Jack and he seems to like it pretty well up there. I don't think it's much different from the places at home. Down here we have altogether a different situation.

I don't have a bit of news, so I will close. Write every chance you get.

Love,
Odis

Tuesday
July 10, 1944

Dear Folks,

How are you by now? I am feeling fine and hope you are the same.

We are really having some hot weather over here, but the nights are pretty cool and I don't have trouble sleeping. They really have lots of grapes around here and I think they will get ripe this month. The figs are as big as an average size lemon and the lemons are the size of our oranges.

I only have 38 missions. I just thought I would drop you a line to let you know I'm ok. Write soon.

Love,
Odis

P. S. I am going to shoot some landings tomorrow and maybe I'll get back to flying soon. It won't take me long to finish when I get started. (One way or the other)
I got a letter from Jack today and he seems to be getting along ok.

The July 10 letter was written five days before he was shot down, and has an ominous statement about finishing his missions, "one way or the other."

CHAPTER 16

Ploesti – July 15, 1944

Early in 1941, after driving the British out of Greece into Crete, the Germans realized the importance of their major oil supply in Ploesti, Romania. England was able to blockade the seas, making Romanian oil and refined products that could be delivered by rail and by barge on the Danube River very important. In May, 1941, the Germans invaded Crete to prevent the British from using the air fields there to bomb Romanian oil-fields.

The first attempt by the allies to damage or destroy the oil refineries was the HALPRO raid in 1942. The mission did almost no damage to the refineries.

The Germans started increasing their defenses in the area. They ringed the Romanian oil fields and refineries with 600 anti-aircraft batteries, along with smaller caliber guns. Several fighter squadrons were also now in place to meet the bombing threat. They built large smoke generators in a ring around the refineries. When word was received that a raid was coming, the smoke was generated covering the entire target area, making the targets impossible to locate.

The next attempt was a raid from Benghazi, Libya, after the Germans left North Africa. This was a low level raid to conserve fuel, and was from a little closer location than the HALPRO raid. This raid was launched in August of 1942 with 177 B-24s flown by experienced crews. Its code name was TITLE WAVE. The raid was less than successful with the loss of 43 aircraft and with minimal damage to the target. Before April, 1944, the 15th Air Force had not made a raid on Ploesti, but had concentrated on airfields, aircraft production facilities, troop support, and sub pens instead. A decision was made to start raids in April to Romania since additional bomb groups and fighter groups were added to the 15th Air Force. The British Air Force also started operations from Italy at the same time, using B-24s and Wellington bombers to drop mines in the Danube River. The mines were effective in slowing the shipment of petroleum products by barge from Romania. The British also flew night raids with pathfinder aircraft dropping flares to illuminate the targets at Ploesti. From April through August 15th made 24 missions to Ploesti with the last one putting the facilities completely out of operation. It has been said that more planes and more men went down over Ploesti than any other target in WWII.

The problem of bombing targets covered by clouds, or concealed by smoke, brought new innovations to solve the problem. The British developed a radar called H2S for aircraft, based on experience with radar operated gunnery and early warning systems. The Americans at M.I.T. developed an improved model called H2X, better known as "Mikey." The H2X was a downward looking radar that sent a pulse of energy, out and the amount of reflected energy would show terrain characteristics. The radar unit was mounted in place of the ball turret, leaving the belly of the plane unprotected.

A PATHFINDER MANUAL OF OPERATION AND TECHNIQUE

PREPARED BY ASSISTANT CHIEF OF STAFF A-3, FIFTEENTH AIR FORC

CONFIDENTIAL

15th Air Force manual for H2X radar.

The radar operator would be seated with the console behind the co-pilot. The radio operator was moved to a position over the bomb bay. The H2X operator coordinated with the bombardier and the visual navigator for a successful bomb drop. The complicated operation of "Mikey" required good training, but could provide very good information for accurate bombing through the obstructions over the target. Some groups started receiving planes equipped with the H2X in March, and by late April, most groups had the units. Planes with these units were called pathfinder planes. By June, the lead planes in all the groups were pathfinder planes.

On July 15, 1944 2nd Lt. Odis Primrose was a co-pilot on the largest mission ever launched against the Ploesti oil complex. All 21 groups of the 15th Air Force participated, sending 607 B-24s and B-17s with 1,526 tons of bombs to the target. This raid was one-third larger than any previous raid, and had a loss of 20 planes. The target for the 450BG was the Romano-Americano Oil Refinery, with 35 bombers and a total bomb load of 80 tons.

Odis, as co-pilot, was part of an experienced, hand selected crew to fly the lead (pathfinder) plane of the four groups of the 47th wing. The other crew members were as follows:

Pilot - Lt. Colonel William Snaith from Dallas, Texas. He was the group operation officer for the 450th, and he was the first person assigned to the 450th as temporary commander when it was organized in Clovis, New Mexico.

Navigator - Captain Jerome Goldvarg from Chicago, Illinois. He was assigned to group headquarters and came over on "Destiny Deb," the first plane to arrive in Manduria, piloted by Lt. Varvil.

Bombardier – 1st Lt. Robert Stricklin from Dallas, Texas. He was originally on the "Shadow" piloted by Captain Grant Caywood. After gaining experience, he became group bombardier.

H2x radar operator – 2nd Lt. George Fritz from River Edge, New Jersey.

Extra Group Navigator – 1st Lt. Earl Tautfest from Kalispell, Montana. He was an observer presumably in training to become a new group navigator. He arrived with Lt. Norbert Bertling's crew in late spring of 1944. Lt. Bertling was killed with another crew on his first mission.

The enlisted crew members were also seasoned personnel with between 35-48 missions each. They are listed as follows:

> Engineer and Top Turret Gunner – T/Sgt. Woodrow "Woody" Allen from Memphis, Tennessee. He was married with one child. Allen was a replacement on the plane "Toni Gayle" in late January or early February, 1944.
> Radio Operator – Staff Sergeant Penn Crawford from West Monroe, Louisiana. He was a member of Lt. Andrew Peterson's crew. He was married and had worked as a bus driver. He had won the Purple Heart Medal for a wound on April 18, 1944.
> Waist Gunner – Staff Sergeant Edward Evans from Bridgeport, Ohio. He was also a member of Lt. Andrew Peterson's crew.
> Ball Turret Gunner – Sergeant John Reid from Chicago, Illinois. He was an original member of Lt. Norbert Bertling's crew, and he was married.
> Aerial Gunner – Staff Sergeant Andrew Johnson, Jr. from North Great Falls, Montana. He was from the "Madam Shoo Shoo Crew" piloted by Lt. Creighton Haupt.

On July 15, 1944, Odis was in a brand new 720th squadron B-24H pathfinder plane #42-51153 named "Strange Cargo" with the latest H2X radar installed. The plane was built in Tulsa by Douglas and had an unpainted, natural aluminum finish. The H2X radar was added as a modification in St. Paul, Minnesota, then sent to Langley Field, Virginia, for overseas assignment. The plane departed June 25, 1944, flying the North Atlantic route through Bangor, Maine and arrived at Manduria on July 2nd. Thirteen days after the plane arrived, it made its first and final mission.

On that fateful day, just after bomb release, a flak shell exploded between the #2 engine (left side) and the bomb bay. A crew member shouted on the interphone that they were hit. The bomb bay then turned into flames. Pilot Snaith tried to control the plane as it nosed over and exploded in a fireball, blowing him out of the plane. Odis and the rest of the crew went down with the plane.

The debriefing upon return of the mission produced statements from aircraft members in Position #3 beside their plane. The following is the account as given by 2nd Lt. Otis K. Andes, recorded in the Missing Crew Report (MACR).

July 16, 1944

"On July 15, 1944, our group was on a mission to bomb the Americano-Romano oil refinery at Ploesti, Romania led by Lt. Colonel William G. Snaith. I was flying as navigator in ship #282 in the #3 position of the lead box of the first attack unit. Lt. Colonel Snaith was flying ship #42-51153 in the lead position of the first attack unit. Up until "Bombs Away" the course was well followed and an excellent formation maintained. On the bombing run, regardless of the extreme closeness of the flak bursts, the flak being heavy, intense and accurate, Colonel Snaith led the group straight to the target and dropped his bombs at 21,500 feet just before a flak burst appeared to explode directly in the bomb bay of his ship. The plane immediately dropped under our plane, then plummeted towards the earth in a mass of flames. I didn't see the burning ship hit the ground because of a very black smoke from the target. I did not see any parachutes leave the ship. Colonel Snaith's ship was last seen at 1020 and the coordinates were 44degrees58'N – 26degrees04'E."

Lt. Andes was shot down and killed July 27, on a mission to Manfried Weiss Armament Works, Budapest, Hungary. He is buried in the Lorraine American Cemetery at St. Avold, France. Several crew members parachuted to safety and became POWs.

A similar statement was given by the nose gunner Cpl. Carl Taylor reporting that he had seen flak burst in the bomb bay causing an explosion of the aircraft. (More information on this event in Chapter 17) He also stated that no parachutes were sighted. Another crewman behind and below the plane said it shook from the hit and dropped out of his sight with the top turret turning into a burned out hole, before exploding.

Research over the last several years has turned up several other first hand accounts of Odis' plane going down. An E-mail correspondence with Louis Eubank in March and April of 2001, provided a vivid description of the event. Louis was a 19 year old flight Engineer/turret gunner on the plane "Myakin." He had only five missions when his crew piloted by Lt. Jack Kath was assigned their first mission to Ploesti. "Myakin" was flying on the right wing of Odis's plane when it exploded in what he called the most horrible and sickening sight he saw during the war. The plane instantly became an orange-red fire ball and disintegrated into a million pieces.

During the mission flak made two holes in his top turret with one piece hitting his .50 caliber machine gun.

When he was interviewed, the tail gunner on "Myakin," Nicholas Altemus, who lives in Port Bolivar, Texas, said he did not see the plane hit from his position, but did see it falling away in flames. Nicholas said a piece of flak came through his turret, hit one of his .50 caliber machine guns, then bounced off the back of his head without hurting him. He said during the bombing runs the fighters would not follow the bombers, so he would normally move back from his turret for protection from flak.

Another eye witness account was in an e-mail from Col. John Jeff in November, 2001. He was a pilot flying number four position about 50 ft under the lead plane when it exploded in his face. He flew his plane through the fireball and received considerable damage from small pieces of the lead plane. He described the flak as being very heavy on the July 15 run from as many as 1,000 88 mm guns.

The official 450th Special Narrative Report No. 105 for July 15th states that 35 B-24s started the mission with two returning due to mechanical problems. The lead plane was hit with flak and went down in flames with a wing off. No chutes were observed. One plane ran out of gas and crashed near the base. The pilot received severe wounds and three other crewmen received moderate wounds. Fifteen aircraft received holes from flak. Eight crewmen received moderate to severe wounds from flak. One aircraft was damaged due to a collapsed nose wheel on landing.

The final results of the mission indicated the bombs dropped short of the target. Flak was intense, very accurate and heavy. The enemy did not field any fighter aircraft since both P-38s and P-15s escorted the bombers to and from the mission. Squadrons of the all Black 332nd fighter group of the Tuskegee Airmen known as the "Black Knights" also escorted some of the groups on that mission. The tail section of their fighter aircraft were painted red, giving them the additional name, "Red Tails."

CHAPTER 17

The Aftermath

The first of the dreaded Western Union telegrams arrived at the Primrose house on July 29, 1944. When Odis' dad walked in with the telegram, his mother looked up and said, "Is it Odis?" His dad answered in the affirmative.

Telegram envelope.

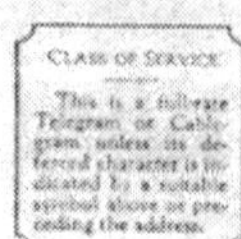
CLASS OF SERVICE
This is a full-rate Telegram or Cablegram unless its deferred character is indicated by a suitable symbol above or preceding the address.

WESTERN UNION

A. N. WILLIAMS
PRESIDENT

SYMBOLS
DL = Day Letter
NT = Overnight Telegram
LC = Deferred Cable
NLT = Cable Night Letter
Ship Radiogram

The filing time shown in the date line on telegrams and day letters is STANDARD TIME at point of origin. Time of receipt is STANDARD TIME at point of destination

BH S 44 GOVT

WASHINGTON D C 317P JUL [illegible] '44

CLYDE C PRIMROSE BOX 573
HEMPHILL TEXAS

THE SECRETARY OF WAR DESIRES ME TO EXPRESS HIS DEEP REGRET THAT YOUR SON SECOND LIEUTENANT CLYDE C PRIMROSE JR HAS BEEN REPORTED MISSING IN ACTION SINCE FIFTEEN JULY OVER ROMANIA IF FURTHER DETAILS OR OTHER INFORMATION ARE RECEIVED YOU WILL BE PROMPTLY NOTIFIED.

ULIO THE ADJUTANT GENERAL
816AM

THE COMPANY WILL APPRECIATE SUGGESTIONS FROM ITS PATRONS CONCERNING ITS SERVICE

Telegram.

This Primrose family was devastated by the telegram, but clung to the hope that Odis had parachuted out of the plane at the last minute and was now a POW. Numerous planes had gone down with no parachutes seen, yet crew members had gotten out and survived.

On August 28, Odis' younger brother, Jack, who was serving in the army in France, sent the following letter home:

Somewhere in France
August 28, 1944

Dear Folks,

I received 2 letters from dad and mom today and one from Boobs girlfriend in England, and last, but not least, appreciated and interesting, 3 from Dot. Keep up the good work.

I am glad the allotment has been changed. Now, I wonder if it will stay the same.

As Daddy said in one of his letters, that I was wondering about what you are doing, thinking and saying, is just right. As you probably have gathered by now, I was in the midst of doing things.

(In fact, I was rolling my pack when I heard the news about Odis.) Since then, I have not had the chance to think of anything and I couldn't do anything to help you or him even if I had the time, so you understand how it is with me. In the meantime, I am doing my designated part in getting this thing over with.

I received the pictures of the girls and Billy this afternoon. I can tell by the shape of his head he is going to be smart, just like me. Ahem. It doesn't seem that he should be such a big boy already.

About that question I answered about the car was when mother asked – well, it doesn't matter now that I am in France anyway. I didn't hear about what happened to Adria and Thel. I will write Dot a letter now.

Love,
Jack

On September 9, Mr. Primrose (Odis' dad) received a letter from the headquarters, Army Air Force, in Washington, as a follow up to the telegram. The letter stated that, after bombing the target, the plane sustained damage from anti-aircraft fire and fell to the earth. The letter also stated that no other details were available, but a continuing search would be made to determine the whereabouts of the missing crew. Due to necessity for military security, the names of the crew members in the plane and the names and addresses of the next of kin would not be furnished at the present time.

Near the end of September, family members living in Houston sent Mr. Primrose a clipping about a 1st Lieutenant Weems, who was shot down over Ploesti. He had just been released from prison camp. Mr. Primrose wrote Lt. Weems asking if he had any information on his son, who went down on the same mission. Since Lt. Weems was in a different group, he did not know Lt. Primrose or have any information about him. Lt. Weems' letter was very comforting and said for them not to lose hope since many crewmen captured are sent to Germany or may be in the hands of the Partisans.

ON CHRONICLE

RELEASED

First Lt. William Z. Weems, Jr., 24, of 2259 Goldsmith, is one of the Houston airmen freed from a Romanian prison camp last week and evacuated to Italy. Lieutenant Weems, pilot of a B-24 Liberator, has been overseas with the Fifteenth A. A. F. since February, Based in Italy, he was reported missing over Romania on his thirty-ninth mission July 15. He was seen to bail out of his plane with nine other members of the crew, but his wife did not know he was a prisoner of war until she received a radiogram from him Sunday informing her that he was "safe and well."

Houston Chronicle article about Lt. Weems.

Houston, Texas
October 23, 1944

Dear Mr. and Mrs. Primrose,

I trust that you good people will forgive me for not answering your good letter sooner, but when the letter arrived, I was still in Italy and my wife thought it best to wait until I arrived home.

I pray to God that by now you have received some good word from your son, but if he is still missing, I want to encourage you as much as possible. It is unbelievable how many men get out of the planes safely. With God's help our whole crew escaped uninjured.

There are many possibilities if the boys bailed out. If they were able to reach Yugoslavia, they may have been rescued by the Partisans and it takes some time to get back to Italy. Many of our boys did this. If they were captured by the Germans then they are in prison in Germany. Ploesti is very near Bulgaria and when a ship is shot up the pilot often tries to make Turkey, but is forced down in Bulgaria. There were many American airmen who are prisoners of the Bulgarian Government.

If you have heard that he is a prisoner of war, please do not worry about the treatment he will receive. All the former prisoners I have talked to were treated very well in fact, we were treated much better than I expected. Do not give up hope as long as your son is reported missing, there is a fine chance that he is safe.

I am sorry that I am unable to give you any more definite information, but since we were in different organizations, we did not know of one another. If you care to send me your son's squadron and group number, I will write to some of my friends in Italy and have them make a personal investigation.

If we can be of any help to you, please let us know at once. Our prayers are that by now you have received some good word.

Respectfully yours,
Lt. and Mrs. William Z. Weems

On November 9, Mr. Primrose received a letter from the Adjutant General at the War Department indicating no new information had been received, but a continuous effort to establish status of personnel who have been reported as missing in action, and any additional information received would be promptly forwarded.

On November 16, Mr. Primrose received another letter from Headquarters, Army Air Force, providing the names of the crew members and of the next of kin with addresses. The names of the next of kin were given in the belief that it would be desirable to correspond with them.

With the hope that they would get information on the disposition of their son, Mr. and Mrs. Primrose started a letter writing campaign to the families of the other crew members. Soon, they started receiving sober and heart rending responses from the other families. The letters came from mothers, fathers, wives, and mothers-in-law of the missing crew.

The first letter came from Irene Stricklin, the mother of the Bombardier. This letter contained a news clipping from the Dallas News about the Pilot, Lt. Col. Snaith's, escape from the exploding plane and his return from Romanian prison camp. He was the highest ranking officer in the prison camp and became camp commander. Shortly after that, a Lt. Col. Gunn from another group was captured and became the new commander, since he had a date of rank over Lt. Col. Snaith. When the German army lost control of the area, Lt. Col. Gunn made a flight in a Romanian fighter plane to Italy and set up an evacuation plan of all POWs. Lt. Col. Snaith was involved in organizing things on the ground in Romania preparing to receive evacuation aircraft.

Mrs. Stricklin's letter gave the first of many comments indicating that only Lt. Col. Snaith survived the plane's being shot down.

Dallas, Texas
November 24, 1944

Dear Mr. and Mrs. Primrose,

I am sending you a clipping from the Dallas News dated October 13th. Lt. Col. Snaith was the pilot on the bomber with our sons and so far, as anyone knows, he is the only one saved. A friend of Robert, Major Caywood, wrote me in September and sent me a ring that Robert had left with him to send to me. He said that Lt. Col. Snaith was the only survivor so when he came home in October, we talked with him. He couldn't tell us much, only what you read in the clipping. Robert was the bombardier. He was on his forty-fifth mission. I don't know the name of the bomber. Major Caywood was pilot of the bomber that Robert went over on. Robert is my youngest son. I have two others, only one in the service. He is at Fairfax Field, Kansas City, Kansas.

If I hear anything at any time, I will let you know.

Mrs. Irene W. Stricklin

Dallas Flier Falls 20,000 Feet As Bomber Splits Over Ploesti

The deadly effectiveness of American air power was learned the hard way by Lt. Col. William G. Snaith, 6502 Midway Road, in faraway Romania following a raid over the Ploesti oil fields.

SNAITH.

Colonel Snaith made a miraculous escape from a Liberator bomber that exploded 20,000 feet over the oil fields and landed amid the wreckage caused by his own comrades. There, lying on the ground trying to get loose from his parachute that had saved his life, Colonel Snaith witnessed the destruction that the mighty giants of the air brought to Romania.

High in the skies over Romania he was leading his wing against the toughest target on that front. The flak was terrific. Suddenly there was a terrific explosion.

Colonel Snaith opened his parachute as he fell from the big bomber that had literally fallen to pieces. He almost lost consciousness and suffered serious burns on the face and body.

Shortly after landing safely Colonel Snaith was taken prisoner by Romanian soldiers and placed in a large school building in the heart of Bucharest where 1,100 other American fliers were confined. Being senior officer, Colonel Snaith was named commander of the prison camp. He was released with other Allied prisoners when Romania surrendered.

Colonel Snaith will not be 29 until January. In 1941 he married Miss Norma Ruth Hill, a Dallas girl. He is now on leave in Dallas.

Colonel Snaith wears the Silver Star, the Distinguished Flying Cross with one Oak Leaf Cluster, the Air Medal with four Oak Leaf Clusters, the Presidential Unit Citation and the Purple Heart.

Dallas News article about Lt. Col. Snaith.

The next letter was from Mr. and Mrs. Evans, who had received word two weeks prior that their son was killed in action. This was the first official information that one of the crew had been killed in action. This letter and the one from Mrs. Stricklin had to have a sobering effect on the Primroses and the other families, since it seemed there was less chance for any survivors. Information discovered later indicated that S/Sgt Evans had fallen clear of the plane, and his body was intact with all his identifications still in his clothes and equipment allowing for immediate identification.

Bridgeport, Ohio
November 24, 1944

Dear Mr. and Mrs. Primrose,

Received your letter stating that your son, Lt. Primrose was on the same plane as my son S/Sgt Edward W. Evans.

We have received word that he had been killed July 15th. My son was Aerial Gunner on the B-24.

The last letter we received from my son, he had 47 missions in.

I am going to write to the nearest of kin of the boys in Edward's crew.

I have two other sons in the service also.

Please accept our sympathy and my God bless you.

Mutual Friends,
Mr. and Mrs. Thomas Evans, Sr.

P.S. If you get anymore news about your son, please write. And here is a snapshot of our son, S/Sgt. Edward W. Evans. If you have a snapshot please send me one. We have a scrapbook of Edward and would like pictures of all in the plane.

Great Falls, Montana
November 26, 1944

Dear Mr. Primrose,

Thanks for your letter of the 22nd instant with expressions of your sympathy during this waiting period of uncertainty.

My son was a gunner on the B-24 Liberator that was shot down over Ploesti, Rumania on July 15 last. I certainly hope that the entire crew was not killed, and we have not given up as yet of seeing our son again.

According to letters from our son Andrew Jr., he must have had nearly 50 missions as he indicated that he would be due for a furlough shortly. He went to Italy with the original 15th Air Force, so I am sure that all members of the crew were seasoned airmen.

I am also planning on writing to each of the nearest of kin and try and keep in touch with them.

I wish to extend my sympathy with the hope that your son and the entire crew will be accounted for and found safe.

With kind regards, I am,
A. N. Johnson, Sr.

The next letter from Mrs. Tautfest indicated she had trouble accepting the fact that her husband was killed, but word from a friend, and a letter from Lt. Col. Snaith was reasonable proof that he died.

Kalispell, Montana
November 28, 1944

Dear Mr. and Mrs. Primrose,

I was so very glad to receive your letter. As yet I haven't received the crew's names or next of kin and have been so anxious to know. Would it be asking too much of you to send me a copy? I would appreciate it.

Have you had answers from the other next of kin yet? My husband was the squadron navigator of the 723rd squadron. I had a letter from him written the night of July 14 and he said Col. Snaith had asked him to fly as his navigator the next day. Like your son, Wayne didn't have a regular crew. He was on his 37th mission and had been in Italy since April 14. (Author's note: Lt. Tautfest was listed as an observer on the flight and believed to be preparing to become the new group navigator.)

On July 15 Snaith was pilot.

Shortly after they were missing I had a letter from one of my friends on the base. He told me that no one escaped from the ship as far as they were able to determine. I wouldn't believe it because the missing crew report didn't seem too gloomy and neither did Major General Twining's letter written in September.

Late in September when the liberated Americans who had been prisoners of war in Rumania came home, one of the boys from here was among them. I went to see him and he told me Col. Snaith had been a prisoner. I then got his address through our Montana Senator and wrote to him. Following is a copy of the letter written October 17.

Dear Mrs. Tautfest,

Having received the letter you wrote my wife upon my return from Rumania and Italy, I shall give all the facts I know concerning your husband.

We did fly together on the July 15th mission with the following events taking place in rapid succession just over the target. The bombs were dropped, flak made a direct hit on one of our gas tanks, the plane was filled with flames and then exploded.

All this happened faster than you read this and while I was still trying to keep the plane flying. The next thing I knew, I was falling freely on my back with the flaming fuselage above me. My parachute landed me safely. I was captured and imprisoned by the Rumanians.

None of the other crew members were brought to the prison camp or ever heard of during the remainder of my stay in Rumania which terminated September 1 when all prisoners were repatriated.

With these facts, I believe it safe to assume that I was the only survivor.

Regretfully,
William G. Snaith

I accepted his word as final. I know that if Wayne had had a matter of seconds he would have been out of the plane. At first I thought I couldn't stand this, but in a way it was a relief to know.

Did the War Dept. ever give you many details? The few letters I have received said very little and the one that came a week ago said no further information had been received. I wondered if all the letters were the same.

Have you heard any word on your son's personal things? I haven't and thought they should be here by now. My friend on the base did send me the money Wayne had left.

I know things like this are hard to read, but I thought you would like to know what I knew about the crew and the flight.

There are so many questions I think of to ask you, but they slip my mind now so you will probably be getting another letter from me.

I hope to hear from you soon and what you hear from others.

Sincerely,
Francile Tautfest

The next letter is from Mrs. Allen, and is very sad. Her husband, T/Sgt. Woodrow Allen, was the only crew member to die, who had a child. She still holds hope, even though Lt. Col. Snaith gave the families little hope.

Pensacola, Florida
November 28, 1944

Dear Mr. and Mrs. Primrose,

Your sweet letter was received yesterday, and words can't express how glad I was to hear from you.

There's not much that I can tell you for the War Department is very slow giving out information and I knew none of the crew members either. That's what makes it so hard to find out anything.

I do know the pilot was the only one that returned to the base there in Italy and he said there was little hope for the other members of the crew, as the Germans got a direct hit in the Bombay and the ship blew up in midair. He was blown clear of the ship and was taken prisoner in Romania. There were no other parachutes seen to open.

I have received no telegram stating my husband was killed, so I still have hopes. That was his forty-ninth mission.

We have a four year old son, and he is the very image of his daddy. As long as he lives I will always be able to see my husband.

We are in Pensacola, Florida with my husband's mother and she asked me to write a few lines for her. She readily understands exactly how you feel, for her son was her heart. We both wish to join you in this time of sorrow.

I have received a letter from Mrs. Ora Mae Crawford, and already she has gotten a telegram stating her husband was killed. That was on November the ninth that she received it. That's the reason we should all have more hopes of our loved ones being safe.

I want you both to know how very sorry I am not being able to give you the information you asked for.

May God bless you always.

Sincerely yours,
Mary K. Allen

Mrs. Blau was the mother of Captain Goldvarg, who was the group navigator and the navigator on their plane July 15th, and wrote the following letter:

Chicago, Illinois

December 2, 1944

Dear Mrs. Primrose,

Received your very lovely letter and before I say anything, I want to thank you for it very much.

I must say you are much better than most of the mothers I know and I must congratulate you for being so brave. Personally, I tried to get in touch with one party here in Chicago, Mrs. Reid and she does not know any more than we do.

We are expecting to hear from one of the boys who was a bombardier in the same group with my boy – he did not go on that mission July 15th. Well, this boy is coming home for Christmas and promised to come in to see us. Yes, he is a Chicago boy. I can assure you, if he can tell us something more definitely, we will let you know.

As far as the War Department is concerned, we have nothing new. Our last letter was just the names of the boys who were on the same mission.

I wish I could say something more encouraging, but I guess we'll just have to wait and hope. I am not going to say any more right now, but let me thank you once more for your very nice letter, and if you hear anything please let us know and I will do the same.

With best wishes to you and your son, I am

Yours truly,
Sarah Blau
My Son's name is Jerome Goldvarg.

West Monroe, La.
December 3, 1944

Dear Mrs. Primrose:

I was very glad to get your letter. It helps lots to hear from some one who had a son or husband on the crew with my husband.

I first got a message that my husband was missing, then on November 9, I received word that he had been killed on July 15th. I'm just wondering if your son is still reported as missing. My husband wasn't flying with his regular crew that day. He was a radio operator and gunner.

I just heard that the pilot was the only one on the crew that was saved. The Germans got a direct hit in the Bombay and the plane blew up in mid-air. The only reason the pilot was saved is that he was blown clear of the ship. He is now back at the field. This information was given me by Mrs. Allen, the wife of one of the men on the crew. Her husband is still reported as missing. I'm just wondering how they know mine is killed.

My husband was on his 47th mission.

If you receive any further information, please let me know.

God bless you always.

Sincerely
Ora Mae Crawford

Mrs. Crawford was the second family member to receive word that her husband had been killed on July 15th. Her husband's body was one of the two that had fallen clear of the plane, and was intact with his identification present. The bodies of the eight remaining crew members were found in the burnt wreckage of the plane, making identification very difficult.

All the families were anxious to get the personal items of their loved ones, as Mrs. Tautfest expressed in her second letter.

Kalispell, Montana
December 10. 1944

Dear Mr. and Mrs. Primrose:

Thank you so very much for the crew list. I hadn't received it yet. I'm wondering if you have heard from the rest of the relatives yet.

I am going to write to Mrs. Stricklin and get the name of the Dallas paper with the story of Snaith and then get a copy. I would like to have one.

Evidently the Evans boy was blown from the ship and they found him. As I understand it, the War Dept. can't declare a person dead, unless they find identification, until a year is up.

I haven't heard anymore from the War Dept. or had any word about Wayne's personal things. I don't care so much about the uniforms, but I would like his bars, wings, shaving kit, wallet, etc. They haven't sent me his air medal either. Wayne only had one ring and that was his college fraternity one and he always wore it. He wore a crash bracelet all the time so I know I won't see those. He sent me some cameos and a friend brought them to the states and mailed them. They came after he was shot down. I have his civilian watch as the army gave him a watch when he finished navigation school.

I was surprised that there was a radar man aboard; it must have been cloudy weather.

Let me know if you hear anymore. I appreciate your letters.

Love,
Francile Tautfest

Bridgeport, Ohio
December 1, 1944

Dear Mr. and Mrs. Primrose,

Received your letter and was very glad to hear from you, and we received the snapshot of your son, Odis.

No, we haven't gotten any of Ed's personal things yet. But, the War Dept. sent us a letter asking if we wanted to know anything to write them and they sent us the address to write. It is Fairfield, Ohio. Did you get a letter asking you the same thing? Maybe there is a place to write there where you live.

You say you have a son in France – is he in the infantry? My son Bob is in France in the infantry.

If we hear any more we will let you know. Let us express our sympathy and God bless you.

We remain your mutual friends,
Mr. and Mrs. Thomas Evans, Sr.

On December 11, Mr. Primrose received this letter from Lt. Col. Snaith, giving the details of the fatal day over Ploesti, and leaving little doubt about the fate of the other members of the crew.

Atlantic City, N.J.

December 12, 1944
My dear Mr. Primrose,

Having received from the War Department a list of the names and addresses of next of kin of those flying with me on that fateful mission of July 15th, I am writing to you to give you an unofficial, but personal account of just what happened.

As you have been informed, our target was an oil refinery at Ploesti Rumania. Our position in flight was that of the Wing Leader; that is we were leading our group which was leading the other three groups of the wing. The mission proceeded normally and as planned until just after the bombs had been dropped over the target, when as we turned away to fly home the plane was hit by flak, (presumably through the bomb bay into the gas tanks) was immediately engulfed in flame and moments later exploded or fell apart leaving me falling about two hundred feet below the flaming fuselage. My only impression of the whole experience was that I tried to hold the plane level, flame shot through the cockpit, the plane started diving and turning to the left so violently that I was unable to leave my seat. I crouched, closed my eyes, expected the end and then found myself out of the plane. Upon falling within four or five thousand feet of the ground, I pulled my cord and made an uneventful parachute descent suffering only flash burns of the face.

Upon being captured by the German and Romanian soldiers they indicated the wreckage and made me understand that some of my crew members had perished in the plane. I was taken to the prison camp at Bucharest, but since no one else was brought in and considering how we were shot down, I assumed that I was the only survivor.

I have learned that in some cases the report of missing in action has been changed to killed in action. That may have been a result of identification by the Rumanian officials in charge of burials who were able to find identification tags and report this information to the Red Cross.

After Rumania capitulated all of the American airmen (over 1,000) including prisoners, hospital patients and those who had not been captured were flown to Italy and shipped home.

This is all I know, but should you care to ask specific questions or should you receive any more news, I would be very glad to hear from you.

Respectfully yours,
William G. Snaith
Lt. Col. AC

River Edge, N.J.
December 15, 1944

Dear Mr. and Mrs. Primrose,

Immediately upon receipt of your letter of the 4th, I had someone I know in Dallas pick up a copy of the newspaper clipping you spoke of and also had her call at the Colonel's residence, where it was reported he was in Atlantic City, N.J. some 150 miles from here.

I telephoned for an appointment at the Green Air Force hotel where he is staying and on Wednesday, December 13 Mr. Fritz and I called upon him and Mrs. Snaith. We also obtained from him the full story of that last mission.

Since he tells me he only wrote you the day before, I know I needn't elaborate on the hopelessness of the situation as far as our boys are concerned. Therefore my friends, while officially as far as the War Dept. is concerned, they are still considered "Missing in Action" and presently will continue in that category until a year and a day from July 15, 1944. We both know that it may be stated as a fact that each of us have lost our sons in the service of his country.

As George was an only child I am sure you can appreciate – having lost one of your own – know how we regard this and the effort it is to write you such a letter. While the knowledge of knowing is heart-breaking, particularly for the mother, I think not knowing would even be worse.

Since the Good Lord has decreed it, thus we must find consolation in that neither could have lost his life in a nobler cause and above all, there was no suffering.

George was also 21 years of age, stood 6'1" and weighed 195 lbs. and had one year at Columbia University. As soon as we receive a reprint of his picture, we will be more than glad to send this to you.

If Clyde's personal belongings (We haven't received George's either except the few small things previously mentioned.) do not come soon, we suggest you write as follows: Army Effects Bureau, Kansas City Quartermaster Depot, 601 Hardesty Avenue, Kansas City, Missouri.

I intend doing so shortly after the first of the year unless I hear from them first. I have been told not to expect too much however, but certainly we are entitled to receive strictly personal things.

Well friends, and I am proud to call you thus, while our correspondence has not developed what we all hoped with our entire beings, it has given the fact and I suppose we must accept the inevitable.

I don't know anything additional to add so will close wishing only the best of everything for you both in the days ahead and especially for your other boy.

Please write whenever you feel up to it and don't forget Clyde's picture.

Sincerely,
George C. Fritz

Christmas holidays were especially hard on the families. Mrs. Rawlings, the mother-in-law of Lt. Tautfest, indicated this in her letter of December 21.

Kalispell, Montana
December 21, 1944

My Dear Mrs. Primrose:

Your letter came this morning. We were so glad for the information. However, I am not going to give it to my daughter until after the holidays. It has been her greatest fear that the plane burst into flames. That was the thing her husband had always feared as he had witnessed the death of a friend that way.

Francile, my daughter, has dreaded the holidays so much. They were so much in love and had been married a year on July 10. They had met at the University of Idaho of which the Lt. was a graduate. She has been feeling better lately as it's been over two months since we had Col. Snaith's letter.

It just doesn't seem right that our lovely boys should have to give their lives. My heart aches now for all the parents of the boys on the front.

Please write us any information that you might receive. So far we haven't had any more information from the government, not even the next of kin.

Where is Lt. Col. Snaith stationed now? Please send his address.

Sincerely,
Mrs. Rawlings

Bridgeport, Ohio
December 26, 1844

Dear Mr. and Mrs. Primrose,

Received your letter and was very glad to hear from you.

We also received a letter from Lt. Col. Snaith. Today (Dec.26) we received two V-mail letters from my son (Bob) in France and we also heard from my other son Charles in England.

Did you receive a "Citation of Honor" from the War Department for your son, Lt. Primrose? We received one. It has Edward's name on it and the date he had been killed.

Well, that's all for now.

Love and good wishes,
Mr. and Mrs. Thomas Evans

On December 30, 1944, Mr. Primrose received an answer to his letter inquiring about his son's personal effects. The Kansas City Quartermaster Depot needed to know if Odis was married, if his mother was living, and if there were any other written instruments indicating who Lt. Primrose designated to receive his property. On January 8, 1945, Mr. Primrose mailed them a copy of Odis' will showing he had been designated as executor of his estate.

The second letter from Mr. Fritz again indicated a note of sadness in that their only son would have had his 22nd birthday the day before.

River Edge, N.J.
January 8, 1945

Dear Mr. Primrose:

Have yours of December 20th and glad to learn that with one exception, you have had word from all families. Seems too bad it could not have been unanimous.

I like the idea expressed in your letter very much and if there is any way I can assist, please feel free to call upon me.

George's new lot of pictures came Friday, so under separate cover, I am glad to send a copy to you and Mrs. Primrose. Hope it gets to you soon and in good shape. Yesterday, January 6th was his birthday when he would have been 22 years of age. I know we don't have to tell you folks we spent it quietly at home wishing things were different, but knowing otherwise.

Please do not forget to send us one of Clyde's pictures as we will be proud to display it alongside our own son's.

If I ever get anywhere near Hemphill, I will make it a point to see you and if you should get up near here, wish you would let me know.

Mrs. Fritz and I send you both our best and trust you will let us hear from you again.

Your friend,
George C. Fritz

Chicago, Ill.
January 8, 1945

Dear Mrs. Primrose:

I really don't know how to start this letter, realizing how wrong I am in not answering your very lovely letter sooner. I want you to know that it is not because I did not want to. It is just we are all just sick about the entire thing – we don't seem to be able to adjust ourselves to the true facts.

As for the Gov. we have not had any further news, he is still missing – but, the letter from Lt. Col. Snaith, which was similar to the one you received tells the very thing we did not want to hear.

Mrs. Primrose, as you said in your last letter, we can but hope for a miracle and so that's just what I am doing.

I will be glad to co-operate with you in anything you suggest. I think it is a lovely thought about getting their photos together and you can count on me to do all I can to help.

And so, here is hoping we may yet hear some good news from our sons. I remain

Very truly yours,
Sarah Blau

P.S. Please don't forget to write again. I'll try to be more prompt.

On January 29, 1945, the Primrose family received the second and final dreaded telegram from the War Department. This was the final closure to what had already been expected.

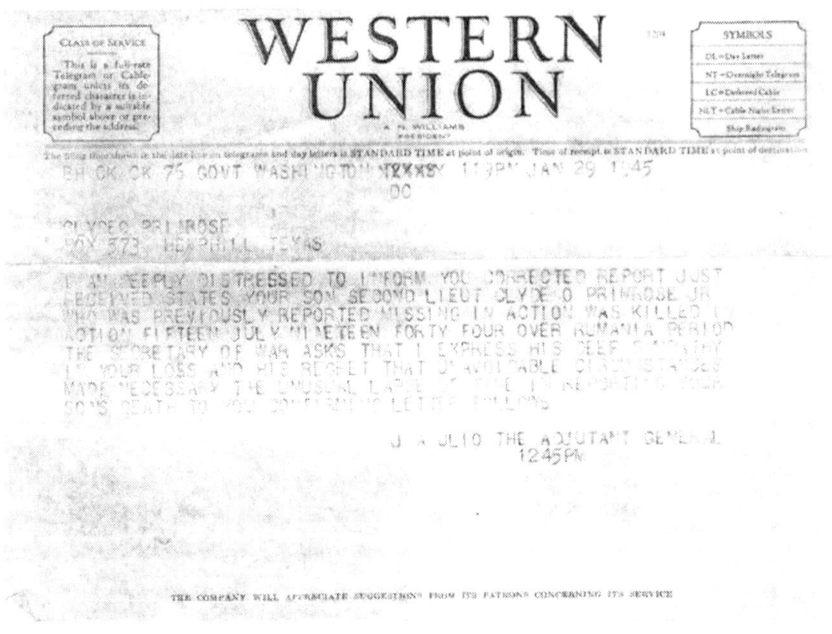

WESTERN UNION

A. N. WILLIAMS
PRESIDENT

CLASS OF SERVICE
This is a full-rate Telegram or Cablegram unless its deferred character is indicated by a suitable symbol above or preceding the address.

SYMBOLS
DL = Day Letter
NT = Overnight Telegram
LC = Deferred Cable
NLT = Cable Night Letter
Ship Radiogram

The filing time shown in the date line on telegrams and day letters is STANDARD TIME at point of origin. Time of receipt is STANDARD TIME at point of destination

WH CK CK 75 GOVT WASHINGTON DC 119PM JAN 29 1945

CLYDE O PRIMROSE
BOX 573 HEMPHILL TEXAS

I AM DEEPLY DISTRESSED TO INFORM YOU CORRECTED REPORT JUST RECEIVED STATES YOUR SON SECOND LIEUT CLYDE O PRIMROSE JR WHO WAS PREVIOUSLY REPORTED MISSING IN ACTION WAS KILLED IN ACTION FIFTEEN JULY NINETEEN FORTY FOUR OVER RUMANIA PERIOD THE SECRETARY OF WAR ASKS THAT I EXPRESS HIS DEEP SYMPATHY IN YOUR LOSS AND HIS REGRET THAT UNAVOIDABLE CIRCUMSTANCES MADE NECESSARY THE UNUSUAL LAPSE OF TIME IN REPORTING YOUR SONS DEATH TO YOU CONFIRMING LETTER FOLLOWS

J A ULIO THE ADJUTANT GENERAL
1245PM

THE COMPANY WILL APPRECIATE SUGGESTIONS FROM ITS PATRONS CONCERNING ITS SERVICE

Killed in action telegram.

When the Primroses got the Killed-in-Action telegram, it was time to exchange the blue star in their window with a gold one. This was an emotional and solemn time for the Primrose family as they placed the gold star in the window. It was an outward sign that they finally accepted that their beloved son and brother, Odis, had been killed.

River Edge, N.J.
January 31, 1945

Dear Mr. Primrose:

Many thanks for yours of the 15th. I am glad George's picture reached you promptly and know one of these days soon I or rather, we will have one of Clyde's.

I suppose you like we, received the final telegram yesterday which only confirmed what we already knew, but perhaps did not want to believe.

By this time we all know how each other feels, particularly we mothers and dads. I am sure God in His infinite wisdom will give us all the strength and courage needed to carry on, so that we as parents will be no less courageous than our sons whose courage is emblazoned in the skies.

Perhaps I didn't mention it before, but when I last saw Colonel Snaith, he told me he was going to write to Italy and see if he could obtain the official picture of the crew.

In a letter received from Mrs. Snaith a few days ago she advised that he had written. If anything further develops along this line I will let you know as I am sure this will fit in nicely with the plans concerning which you have previously written me.

We both send our best to you and Mrs. Primrose and hope you will write again when you have an opportunity.

Sincerely,
Your friend
George Fritz

Mr. Primrose received the follow-up letter after the KIA telegram on February 6th. General Ulio, Adjutant General of the War Department, wrote to confirm the telegram regarding the death of Lt. Primrose on July 15, 1944. The last paragraph stated:

> "I realize the burden of anxiety that has been yours since he was first reported missing in action and deeply regret the sorrow this later report brings you. May the knowledge that he made the supreme sacrifice for his home and country be a source of sustaining comfort."

After receiving the KIA telegram, Mr. Primrose inquired again about the disposition of Lt. Primrose's personal effects. On the 8th, he received word that the personal effects would be shipped in two containers shortly. When the items arrived, they contained a foot locker, field jacket, shirts, pants, caps, underwear, watch, various insignias, and miscellaneous items.

On February 6, the family received a card from General Marshall, the Chief of Staff of the Army.

> "General Marshall extends his deep sympathy in your bereavement. Your son fought valiantly in a supreme hour of his country's need. His memory will live in the grateful hearts of our nation."

Oh February 14, 1945, a letter was received from General Giles, Deputy Commander of the Army Air Forces, expressing his sympathy for the loss to the members of the family in their bereavement. This letter was much more than the usual form letter sent out to families of men killed in action. His second paragraph gave individual details of his military service:

> "Information has reached me that Lt. Primrose had experience as an enlisted man which he used to advantage while he was in training in Lubbock Army Air Field, where he was appointed flight officer. The promotion he later received attests the high regard superiors had for his ability as an airman. The skill and leadership he possessed helped him to develop into an excellent officer of whom you can be proud."

The next letter on March 2, from Henry Stinson, Secretary of War, stated that he had been requested by the President, to inform the family that their son had been awarded the Purple Heart posthumously. The last two paragraphs state:

> "The medal which you will receive shortly is of slight intrinsic value, but rich in the tradition for which Americans are so gallantly giving their lives. The Father of our country, whose profile and coat of arms adorn the medal, speaks from it across the centuries to the men who fight today for the proud freedom he founded.
>
> Nothing the War Department can do or say will in any sense repair the loss of your loved one. He has gone, however, in honor and this goodly company of patriots. Let me, in communicating to you the country's deep sympathy, also express to you its gratitude for his valor and devotion."

A letter of sympathy was received from W. Lee O' Daniel, Senator from Texas, on March 2. Later, a letter came from H. H. Arnold, Commanding General, Army Air Forces stating, "With the coming of Memorial Day we will again all be mindful of the debt to those of the Air Forces who gave their lives for our country."

From March through October of 1945, numerous letters came in dealing with the $10,000 insurance policy, government benefits available, and any pay due Lt. Primrose. The estate was due the balance of his pay, plus six month gratuity pay, less $33.75 due the government for meals, leaving a total of $1,696.35, which was paid in October, 1945.

On October 17, 1946, a final letter came from the Kansas City Quartermaster Depot that an additional item of Lt. Primrose had been located and would be forwarded as soon as the current address could be confirmed. Over two years after his death on November 3, 1946, a small package arrived containing a 1st Lieutenant Bar, the last of his personal effects.

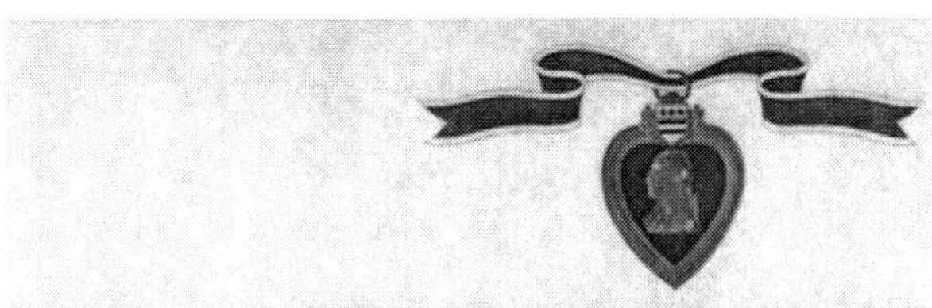

THE UNITED STATES OF AMERICA

TO ALL WHO SHALL SEE THESE PRESENTS, GREETING:

THIS IS TO CERTIFY THAT
THE PRESIDENT OF THE UNITED STATES OF AMERICA
PURSUANT TO AUTHORITY VESTED IN HIM BY CONGRESS
HAS AWARDED THE

PURPLE HEART

ESTABLISHED BY GENERAL GEORGE WASHINGTON
AT NEWBURGH, NEW YORK, AUGUST 7, 1782
TO

Second Lieutenant Clyde O. Primrose, Jr., A.S.No. 0-1703131,

FOR MILITARY MERIT AND FOR WOUNDS RECEIVED
IN ACTION

resulting in his death July 15, 1944.

GIVEN UNDER MY HAND IN THE CITY OF WASHINGTON
THIS 23rd DAY OF March 1945

IN GRATEFUL MEMORY OF

Second Lieutenant Clyde O. Primrose, Jr., A.S.No. 0-1703131,

WHO DIED IN THE SERVICE OF HIS COUNTRY ~~AT~~

in the Mediterranean Area, July 15, 1944.

HE STANDS IN THE UNBROKEN LINE OF PATRIOTS WHO HAVE DARED TO DIE

THAT FREEDOM MIGHT LIVE, AND GROW, AND INCREASE ITS BLESSINGS.

FREEDOM LIVES, AND THROUGH IT, HE LIVES—

IN A WAY THAT HUMBLES THE UNDERTAKINGS OF MOST MEN

PRESIDENT OF THE UNITED STATES OF AMERICA

Certificate from the president.

Be It Known That

The State of Texas

Places the Name of

CLYDE O. PRIMROSE, JR.

upon the roll of those who have rendered the highest service. The loss of his life in the service of his country in World War II will always be remembered by those who love freedom.

In humble recognition of his sacrifice, the Legislature of Texas, in the name of its people, has directed me to acknowledge the debt of free men to him who gave his life that others might live, and commend him to the living memory of Texans everywhere.

In Testimony Whereof, *I have hereunto signed my name and caused the Seal of State to be affixed at the City of Austin this the 11th day of May A.D. 1946.*

By the Governor:

Secretary of State

Governor of Texas

Certificate from the state of Texas.

CHAPTER 18

Identification and Return of Remains

It was early 1948, and the Primrose family was very disturbed that after four years, they had received no information concerning the location of the remains of their son. A letter from Mr. Fritz encouraged them to ask for additional information.

River Edge New Jersey
January 26, 1948

Dear Mr. and Mrs. Primrose,

It has been quite some time since I have written you and I sincerely hope this finds both of you well and that like ourselves time has eased the pain of our losses, although we can never forget.

I don't want to revive unpleasant memories, but I did once promise to keep in touch with you concerning any information I received from the War Department concerning George, so here goes.

Recently I inquired relative to his grave location, if any, and was advised there was no record, but in the past week was informed that he is now in the United States Military Cemetery, Neuville-en Condroz, Belgium and was wondering if perhaps you folks received similar information.

Belgium in Western Europe is a long way from Rumania in the eastern section and it sort of makes you wonder of course if Clyde and George are together. It sort of adds up and begins to appear logical.

The best of everything from Mrs. Fritz and myself. If you will drop me a few lines, I certainly would appreciate it.

Sincerely,
George C. Fritz

Based on the information from Mr. Fritz, Mr. Primrose wrote the following letter in May, 1946.

Hemphill, Texas
May 9, 1948

Richard B. Combs
Major QMC Memorial Division
Dear Sir,

We have never heard whether or not our son, killed over Rumania, was buried there or not. I'm enclosing a copy of a letter written by you to the parents of George H. Fritz, who was killed on the same plane with my son, 2ndLt. Clyde O. Primrose, Jr., ASN 0-1703131.

Please advise us concerning our son, if and where he is buried.

Very truly yours,
Clyde O. Primrose

On May 25, 1948 Mr. Primrose received an answer to his letter from the Memorial Division.

25 May 1948

Dear Mr. Primrose:

Your letter pertaining to the remains of your son, the late Second Lieutenant Clyde O. Primrose, Jr., has come to my attention.

Although no conclusive information is available as to the recovery and identification of the remains of your son, remains have been disinterred from the Cemetery of Berceni-Prahova, Rumania, and re-interred in the United States Military Cemetery, Neuville-en-Condroz, Belgium, which may be those of your loved one. An investigation is now being conducted in order to determine the identity of those remains. Upon the conclusion of this investigation, you will be informed of the results.

I wish to inform you that some of your son's crew members have been identified and others are still in the process of investigation.

May I extend my sympathy in your great loss.

Sincerely yours,
Richard C. Coombs
Major, QMC
Memorial Division

No other significant correspondence was received from the government until May 4, 1951. Not receiving anything positive about their son's remains, for over six years after his death, was a painful experience.

4 May 1951
QMGMF 293
Primrose, Clyde O., Jr.
SN 0-1 703 131

Mr. Clyde O. Primrose
P. O. Box #573
Hemphill, Texas

Dear Mr. Primrose:

This office desires to furnish you information concerning the recovery and identification of the remains of your son, the late Second Lieutenant Clyde O. Primrose.

According to Department of the Army records and reports received from overseas Command, your son was one of eleven crew member manifested aboard a B-24 type aircraft, serial number 42-51153, which failed to return from a combat mission to Ploesti, Rumania, on 15 July 1944. This plane is reported to have exploded when hit by flak just after the bomb run. The force of the explosion blew the pilot clear of the plane, he survived and subsequently returned to the United States. The remaining ten crew members, including your son, were killed in the crash.

Rumanian records indicate that an American aircraft crashed in the Berceni area on 15 July 1944 and the remains of the crew members were interred in the civilian cemetery at that place.

At a later date, these remains were recovered by units of our American Graves Registration Service and removed to a United States Military Cemetery for processing through an identification laboratory in an effort to establish individual identifications. The remains were examined by an accredited anthropologist, utilizing advanced scientific and technical procedures, and it was possible to individually identify all of the deceased crew members.

The identification of the remains of your son is based upon favorable comparison of physical and dental characteristics of the remains as compared to the information on file for your son with the Department of the Army.

The remains of your son are presently casketed and being held in an overseas mortuary pending disposition in accordance with your instructions; either for return to the United States or for permanent burial in an American Military Cemetery overseas.

There are enclosed informational pamphlets regarding the Return of World War II Dead Program, including a Disposition form on which you may indicate your desires in this matter. Upon receipt of the properly completed form, you may be assured that the Department of Army will make every effort to comply your instructions as indicated thereon.

In order that this office may take immediate action toward the final disposition of the remains of your son, it is urged that you complete the enclosed form "Request for Disposition of Remains" and mail it to this office in the self-addressed envelope which requires no postage.

Sincerely yours,
James B. Clearwater
Colonel, QMC
Chief, Memorial Division

Upon requesting the remains to be returned, the family was notified by letter that they were in route to the U. S. with delivery to Starr Funeral Home in Hemphill, Texas. A telegram was received by the Funeral Home with instruction on the receiving of the remains.

BH N CK GOVT PD BNA BROOKLYN NY 321 PM JULY 12/51
STARR FUNERAL HOME
DLR AND REPORT ANY CHGS
HEMPHILL TEX.

PLEASE BE ADVISED REMAINS OF 2 LT CLYDE O PRIMROSE JR WITH MILITARY ESCORT DEPARTS JERSEY CITY VIA B&O RR TRAIN 200 PM EST ON MON 16 JULY 51 ARRIVES BRONSON TEX VIA AT&SF RR TRAIN 201 AT 1126 AM EST ON WED 18, JULY 51 COST OF TRANSPORTATION FROM BRONSON TO HEMPHILL TO BE PAID FROM GOVERNMENT FUNDS PD LETTER WITH INSTRUCTIONS REGARDING PAYMENT WILL FOLLOW PLEASE ARRANGE TO ACCEPT REMAINS AT RR STATION AND NOTIFY NOK

OF TIME AND DATE OF ARRIVAL NOK IS CLN MR CLYDE O PRIMROSE FATHER POST OFFICE BOX 573 HEMPHILL TEX . . .
(MAJOR H O YOUNG CHIEF AMERICAN GRAVES REGISTRATION BRANCH NEW PORT OF EMBARKATION.)
339P

The remains of Lt. Primrose arrived at noon July 18, 1951, seven years and three days after his death. A military escort delivered the casket to the Primrose home. The decision was made to bury Lt. Primrose in Jasper, since the family was in the process of moving there. The funeral service, however, was conducted at the Hemphill Church of Christ at 2:30 on July 19, 1951. The remains were then transferred to Jasper, Texas, where a military service was conducted by the American Legion. All his immediate family, along with many of his extended family and friends stood silently, as the three volley salute was given. After the sound of the rifles had subsided, the final taps were played. Odis was home and in his final resting place, only a few miles from where he was born.

Casket at Primrose home.

Odis' brothers and sisters after the funeral.

CHAPTER 19

Questions Answered

Some fifty years after Lt. Primrose died, many questions still lingered as to why it took so long to bring his remains back home. The youngest brother, Bill Primrose, wrote to Lt. Col. Snaith in 1997 for any additional information that he could supply.

Col. Snaith did not shed any light on why it took so long for the Government to act, but did offer more details on the fatal flight. He said that the plane was a brand new B-24H with a radar system. It was flown by him and his group staff the day before to see if everything was operational. He said that, during the mission, Odis had performed his duties as co-pilot in a professional manner. He had checked the gunners by intercom, clearing them to fire their guns, advised them when they started to climb to bombing altitude, and checked periodically that they were on oxygen. When the flak shell hit, he and Odis unbuckled their seat belts to prepare to bail out when he lost control of the plane.

In 1999, the 96 year old mother of Odis, Leavie Primrose, was still bothered by the death of her firstborn son. She asked me (the author) to assist in obtaining additional information by requesting a copy of the Missing Air Crew Report (MACR#6995) and the Individual Deceased Personnel File. The copy of the MACR arrived on microfilm and was very hard to read due to the age of the original document.

The only new information was the account by 2nd Lt. Otis Andes and Cpl. Carl Taylor who were flying in the same box as the lead plane. Lt. Andes was later killed on a raid July 27 to the Manfred Weiss Works in Budapest, Hungary.

The receipt of the two hundred and five page Individual Deceased Personnel File opened up a completely new chapter in the recovery of Lt. Primrose's remains, giving an understanding of the 7 year delay. (Author's note: My military experience with Graves Registration was invaluable in understanding the terminology used in the file.)

The story begins on June 24, 1944, when 2nd Lt. Salinger of the 721st Squadron and his crew flew aircraft #21 on a mission to Ploesti. MACR #6367 records the other crew members as Capt. MacQueen, 1st Lt. Gottlieb, 2nd Lt. Vartanian (this was Vartanian's first mission), and the enlisted crew as Tandy, Bott, Panos, Brooks, Owens and Weishaar. The MACR contains this description of the incident by Capt. MacQueen:

> "Capt. MacQueen's plane was hit by flak immediately after dropping bombs on target at Ploesti, Rumania on 24 June 1944. This flak hit did considerable damage to the rear part of the plane and disabled rudder and elevator control. The bail-out alarm was sounded and the order to bail out was given over intercom system, but Capt. MacQueen does not know whether either of these systems was in working order.
>
> Plane went into a diving left turn out of control. Pilot was attempting to control plane with ailerons. While in this dive, the plane received another direct flak hit in the nose of the plane blowing up the nose turret completely and setting the hydraulic fluid in the nose on fire. When fire blazed into the cockpit both Capt. MacQueen and Lt. Salinger abandoned the cockpit for purpose of escape through the bomb bay doors. Upon arriving in the bomb bay it was discovered that the hydraulic system had been damaged so that it was impossible to open the bomb doors hydraulically. Immediately afterwards, the plane went into a vertical spin and five members of the crew – pilot, bombardier, navigator and engineer – were thrown on the floor and were unable to move, so that it was impossible to reach the emergency bomb bay door crank to open the door. At no time after the first hit did anyone in the forepart of the plane know anything about the situation in the waist and tail turret.
>
> After spinning for an appreciable length of time the right front bomb bay door on which Capt. MacQueen and Lt. Gottlieb were lying, gave way so that those two members were thrown clear of the plane and successfully parachuted to the ground. Capt. MacQueen estimated that at the time he was thrown from the plane, it was at an altitude of about 3,000 feet. Capt. MacQueen and Lt. Gottlieb saw no other parachute, but the airplane was observed to spin into the ground and explode and burn. Captain MacQueen does not know whether or not any crew members in the waist of the plane escaped prior to the plane entering the spin.

> Due to the wind drift, both Capt. MacQueen and Lt Gottlieb landed approximately one-quarter of a mile from the place where the plane struck the ground, and were immediately picked up by the Rumanian soldiers. The Rumanian and German authorities to whom he talked at a later time refused to let either Capt. MacQueen or Lt. Gottlieb visit the scene of the crashed plane. They were subsequently imprisoned in Lagarul De Priszoneri No.13 in Bucuresti, Rumania, and no members of their crew ever appeared at that prison during the period of their imprisonment. Capt. MacQueen reported the remaining members of the crew as missing-in-action to the senior American officer in the prison camp and to Hqs. of the 15th AF when he was liberated and returned to Bari, Italy.
>
> Capt. MacQueen is of the opinion that due to the difficulty of escape from Rumania, other members of the crew must not have survived or they would have shown up in the prison. He is positive that the nose turret gunner was destroyed when flak hit the nose of the plane. He is also confident that those three members on the crew who were in the bomb bay with him during the spin did not get out before the plane crashed."

Lt. Salinger's crew members were buried by the Romanian authorities in the nearby village of Berceni in Prahova providence.

Three weeks later Lt. Primrose's plane went down in the same area, and the crew was also buried in the Berceni Cemetery. On December 11, 1944, an early U.S. investigating detachment arrived in the area to investigate the location of the missing airmen. The Berceni Police Chief provided the location of the graves and what identification they found. The bodies of Evans and Crawford were identified since they fell away from the plane. The eight bodies in the wreckage were burned and no identification was made.

The recovery of remains did not start until the 2621st Quartermaster Graves Registration Detachment made their way to the Berceni area in Aug, 1946. The job of the graves registration units was a massive undertaking, with over 2,500 crewmen who died over Rumania. On August 20, 1946, the bodies were disinterred and moved to a U.S. Military Cemetery in Sinaia, Rumania, for reburial. The Sinaia Cemetery was used as a central collection point with 355 graves at the time the crews were reburied.

The next step was the disinterment in January, 1947, to remove all remains to the central identification point at Neuville-en-Condroz, Belgium. The collection point was used for remains from all over Europe. The remains were evaluated for future identification. The remains of Lt. Primrose consisted of an incomplete fractured skeleton, along with some fragments of clothing and identification papers. The remains were missing hands, feet and, major bones in the arms. Clothing items consisted of remnants of a Jacket, trousers with suspenders, drawers, parachute harness, fleece lined flying suit, and flak vest. Identification items were found in a torn, stained and charred wallet. The wallet contained parts of Lt. Primrose's ID card, calling card, PX card, and finance receipt. In 1951, authorization was give to destroy all of these personal items, because they were not presentable for returning to the next of kin. This is an army policy to prevent additional grief to the family.

On March, 1947, his remains were reburied in a casket at Plot V, Row 6, Grave #131 marked with a temporary wooden cross. The other crew members of both planes were also reburied at this time. A joint Protestant and Catholic service was conducted.

The final identification process on the crews of Lt. Primrose and Lt. Salinger, by a Dr. Simonin, a Professor of Forensic Medicine at the University of Strasburg, was started in August of 1949. The investigation of the remains was hindered due to the intermingling of the remains of the two crews when disinterred at Berceni. Dr. Simonin, after a study of the remains, issued his finding on the 18 crew members. The remains of Lt. Primrose was identified as X-4981 (X for yet unidentified) and contained portions of his identification papers, but some of the teeth of a Sgt. Brooks, X-5015, and Reid, X-8214, were found with Lt. Primrose's remains. He wrongly concluded from Brook's teeth that the remains of Lt. Primrose were those of Brooks.

The original identifications by Dr. Simonin had so many unsolved problems that a Dr. Tandy was requested to do an anthropological study of all eighteen remains simultaneously in February of 1950. Comparing available dental charts, physicals, and past flight physical records, to the cranial fragments with teeth that had been incorrectly placed with Brooks, he made a positive identification of Lt. Primrose's remains. On November 16, 1950, the remains were placed in a casket in preparation for shipment to the U. S. when approved. A Board of Review for identification of unknown dead overseas met on March 29, 1951, and approved the identification of Lt. Primrose, and arrangement was made for shipment.

The remains of Capt. Goldvarg, 1st Lt. Stricklin, S. Sgt. Crawford, Sgt Reid, Lt. Tautfest, and Lt. Fritz were all buried in the Ardennes American Cemetery, Neuville, Belgium. The remains of the eight members of Lt. Salinger's crew were returned to the U. S. and buried in Jefferson Barracks, Mo. Cemetery on June 28, 1951, seven years after they were shot down.

EPILOGUE

The Primrose family has had a long history of serving in the service to our country. Jack, Odis' younger brother, finished his WWII Army service in Europe and returned home. One son-in-law served in the Navy during the latter part of WWII. Three other sons-in-law served during the Korean conflict, and two served during peace time. William "Bill" Primrose, (called Billy Boy by Odis) the youngest son, served during the Viet Nam conflict. Three grandsons also served during peace time and one great-grandson served in Iraq. This represents twelve family members, who served through four wars, not to mention those at home, who anxiously awaited their safe return.

In 1952 1st Lt. Carl Walker, the bombardier on Odis' original crew and his wife came to Jasper from Houston, Texas, on a Sunday to visit with the Primrose family. Lt. Walker was married before he joined the service. The visit lasted several hours and was very comforting to the family. He told them that Odis was a fine young man, liked by all and they could be very proud of him. Lt. Walker's wife mentioned that Odis was a sweet and considerate man. As an example of Odis' consideration for others, she said that he volunteered to take guard duty so that the married men could spend time with their wives the night before they shipped out. They considered Odis an all around good guy.

Odis' youngest brother wrote a song for the 200th anniversary of our nation in 1976 in honor of his brother, Odis.

Freedom's Hope
By William Primrose

My heart's a swellin' as I behold
Old Glory unfurled, so proud, so bold.
Now hear the anthem, everyone rise.
It's happened again, I've got tears in my eyes.

Some say a patriot's a thing of the past.
I say no! And I cling steadfast.
To the memory of our fathers who were here before.
Who lived with a hope for freedom evermore.

So lift up your eyes, thank God for our land.
Happy birthday, America, from a very thankful man.

Our brother's gone to glory with wings upon his chest.
His crew was young and brave, they were America's best.
They flew that day through hell, a hundred planes or more.
They died with a hope for freedom evermore.

Some say a patriot's a thing of the past.
I say no! And I cling steadfast.
To the memory of our fathers who were here before.
Who died with the hope for freedom evermore.

So lift up your eyes, thank God for our land.
Happy birthday, America! May you always stand!

On July 4th of 1993, three of the sisters sang this song at a July 4th program in aptly named Liberty, Texas.

In 2000, I (the author) while researching the material for this book, contacted Colonel Robert Gideon, who was the group commander in July, 1944, and the roommate of Lt. Col. Snaith. I asked him for a summary of the group training before going overseas. Over fifty years after the events, he graciously responded with great detail.

16 October 2000

Dear Clarence:

With what memory remains, I'll try to answer your questions about B-24 training. When I got to B-24 training, I already had two years flying experience in single and twin planes. When I arrived in Alamogordo, my flying time in B-24's was about 100 hours. This was much more than our normal pilots.

As I remember the training regimen, there was primary flying at civilian schools supervised by Air Corps Officers (2 each) and a few mechanics. This lasted about 3 months. From there they went to basic training in BT-17s for another 3 or 4 months. From there to advanced school in single and twin engine planes. It appears that your brother-in-law got his wings at Waco then went to Advanced at Lubbock.

Then they went to combat aircraft training, probably at Ft. Worth for B-24s after Ft. Worth there were other training bases for B-24s before pilots were sent to combat units like the 450th.

We were at Alamogordo for about 4 months for formation, bombing navigation. There were 4 combat squadrons plus headquarters. Bill Snaith (now deceased) was Director of Operations, I was Deputy Commander and later Commander. I flew 4 missions over Ploesti.

From N. M. we went to staging at Hastings, NE, where we got new A.C, clothes, etc. Then to Natal Brazil, via Florida across the southern Atlantic to Senagal, to Libya, then to Manduria. The crews got a lot of flying experience from NM to Italy. We trained in Manduria from November to January, then flew a few "easy" combat missions starting in January, 1944.

I hope this helps you.
Sincerely, Bob Gideon

This letter represents the last correspondence dealing with the service of 2nd Lt. Primrose. Odis, always concerned about his family, had taken out a $10,000 G.I. Insurance policy naming his mother as beneficiary. She chose to take monthly checks for as long as she lived rather than a lump sum. She continued to receive the monthly checks of $47.00 for the rest of her 99 years. The money was invaluable in the forties, and very helpful after retirement. At some point in time, the amount was upgraded to $75 per month.

2nd Lt. Clyde Odis Primrose was awarded the following medals:

Good Conduct Medal
European-African-Middle Eastern Campaign Medal
Air Medal with three Oak Leaf Clusters
Purple Heart (Posthumously)

Author's Note: It is ironic that in 1943 I lived eleven miles from Lt. Primrose's sixth youngest sister Dixie, but never saw her until both our families moved to Jasper, Texas. We were married in 1955. We have two children, four grandchildren, and one great-grandchild. We live in Lumberton, Texas.

Below is a list of the other members of Odis' family and their status as of the date this book:

Odis' Dad, Clyde Primrose, died at the age of 83 in 1986.

Odis' Mother, Leavie McDonald Primrose, died at the age of 99 in 2003.

Jack completed his tour of duty in the Army in 1946, returned home and married Wanda Beard. They had one son, Paul Odis Primrose. Jack passed away in 1980 with cancer. Wanda lives in Austin.

Dorothy (Dot) married Morris Istre. They have two children and two grandchildren. They live in Baytown, Texas.

Leatrice (Lily) married Ralph Carr, Jr. and had two children and four grandchildren. Ralph passed away in his sleep in 1999, and Leatrice died from Parkinson's Disease in 2000.

Faye married Dick Berry and has one daughter, four grandchildren, and nine great grandchildren. She is divorced and lives in Liberty, Texas.

Frances married Ray E. Carder, and had five children, nineteen grandchildren, and four great grandchildren. Ray passed away in 2001 from cancer. Their oldest son, Mike, passed away in 2007 with cancer. She lives in Liberty, Texas.

Shirley is currently married to Paul Wilson, and lives in Hamshire, Texas. She has three children and four grandchildren from her previous marriage to Lynn Smith.

Mary Jane married James Beard. They have two children and two grandchildren. They live in Spring, Texas.

William (Bill) and his wife, Jean, live in Lake Jackson, Texas. They had 3 children and two grandchildren. Their oldest son, Scot passed away in 1995. Bill was born only four months before Odis was killed.

Pansy Etta, who was not born until 2 years after Odis was killed, married Rick Johnson, and has two children and one grandchild. She is divorced and lives in Lumberton, Texas.

BIBLIOGRAPHY

BOOKS

Birdsall, Steve, *Log of the Liberators*, Doubleday, 1973
Bowman, *B-24 Liberator 1939-46*, Patrick Stephen, Ltd, 1989
Childers, Thomas, *Wings of Morning*, Addison-Wesley Publishing Co., 1996
Colley, David P., *Safely Rest*, Berkley Publishing Group, 2005
Cubbins, William R., *The War of the Cottontails*, Algonquin Books, 1989
Currier, Donald R., *50 Mission Crush*, Burd Street Press, 1993
Fagan, Vincent F., *Liberator Pilot*, California Aero Press, 1991
Fili, William J., *Passage to Valhalla*, Filcon Publishers, 1999
Forman, Wallace R., *B-24 Nose Art Name Directory*, Specialty Press, 199
Glen, Alexander, *Target Danube*, The Book Guild Ltd, 2002
Griffin, Thomas P., *Fast Track to Manhood*, Trafford Publishing, 2003
Kinzey, Bert, *B-24 Liberator*, Squadron/Signal Publications, 2000
Khon, Leo J., *Flight Manual for B-24 Liberator*, Aviation Publications, 1989
McGuire, Melvin W., *Bloody Skies*, Yucca Tree Press, 1993
Muirhead, John, *Those Who Fall*, Random House, 1986
Newby, Leroy W., *Target Ploesti*, Presidio Press, 1983
Pardini, Albert L., *The Legendary Secret Norden Bombsight*, Schiffer Publishing Ltd. 1999
Raiford, Neil Hunter, *Shadow*, McFarland & Company, Inc., 2004
Rust, Kenn C., *Fifteenth Air Force Story*, Sun Shine House, 1976
Stout, Jay A., *Fortress Ploesti*, Casemate, 2003
Turner, Dave, *450th Bomb Group(H)*, Turner Publishing Co., 1996

VIDEOS

Flying The Bombers – B-24 Liberator, American Sound & Video
The B-24 Story, American Sound & Video
Ploesti! B-24 at War Series I, American Sound & Video

RELATED AIRCRAFT MUSEUMS

United States Air Force Museum, Dayton, Ohio
Lone Star Flight Museum, Galveston, Texas
Commemorative Air Force Museum (Formally Confederate A.F.), Midland, Texas
8th Air Force Museum, Barksdale Air Force Base, Shreveport, La.
Pima Air Museum, Tucson, Az.
Castle Air Museum, Castle, La.
Pueblo Weisbrod Aircraft Museum, Pueblo, Co.

SOURCE FOR GOVERNMENT DOCUMENTS

National Archives and Records Administration
8th Street and Pennsylvania Ave.
Washington, D. C. 20408
(Missing crew reports and other military records)

National Personnel Records Center
9700 Page Blvd.
St. Louis, Mo. 63132
(Servicemen's Personnel Records – 75% to 80% lost in 1973 from fire)

Air Force Historical Research Agency
600 Chennault Circle
Maxwell AFB, AL 36112-6424
(Missing air crew reports & depository of WWII unit records)

U. S; Total Army Personnel Command
200 Stovall St.
Alexandria, Va.
(Individual deceased personnel files)

USEFUL WEBSITES

WWII Stalag Luft & POW Camps of WWII
http://Dotstar.US/POW2/
(List of prisoners in German P.O.W. camps.)

Department of Veterans Affairs Nationwide Graves Locator
http://Gravelocator.cem.Va.Gov
(List of men buried in National Cemeteries)

American Battle Monuments Commission
www.abmc.gov
(List of Americans buried in U.S. cemeteries on foreign soil and memorial to those missing in action.)

450th Bomb Group Official web site
www.450thBG.com
(List of 450thBG personnel, crew pictures, aircraft information, etc.)

NOTE: Most combat groups from WWII maintain active web sites that can be found with a search engine.

Composite drawing of “Strange Cargo” by S. A. Berry

CPSIA information can be obtained at www.ICGtesting.com
Printed in the USA
LVOW121117220513

334995LV00003B/391/P